# AN INTRODUCTION TO THE SCIENCES OF COMMUNICABLE DISEASES

PROF. (DR.) NITISH BHATIA

Made with ♥ on the Notion Press Platform
www.notionpress.com

Dedicated to My Wife, Anita Bhatia

Your Support has been my Lifeline

# Contents

# Contents

# Preface

Welcome to "An Introduction to the Sciences of Communicable Diseases". This book serves as a comprehensive guide to understanding the intricate world of communicable diseases, offering a blend of historical context, scientific principles, public health strategies, and ethical considerations.

Communicable diseases have shaped human history, from the devastating plagues of antiquity to the ongoing battle against emerging pathogens in our modern era. In recent times, events such as the COVID-19 pandemic have underscored the critical importance of preparedness, prevention, and global cooperation in combating infectious threats.

The journey through this book begins with an exploration of the fundamental concepts, definitions, and classifications of communicable diseases, setting the stage for a deeper dive into their historical impact and major pandemics. From there, we delve into the realms of microbiology, examining the diversity of microorganisms, their ecological roles, and the tools used to study them.

Understanding the intricacies of microbial structure, function, and transmission is essential for grasping the mechanisms underlying disease spread and immune response. Chapters dedicated to immunology shed light on the body's defense mechanisms, the role of vaccines, and the concept of herd immunity in disease control.

Epidemiology takes center stage as we explore outbreak investigation, disease surveillance, and the implementation of prevention and control strategies. Through case studies, we examine successful disease eradication programs and highlight the pivotal role of public health in safeguarding communities.

Furthermore, this book emphasizes the importance of international collaboration and ethical considerations in addressing global health threats. As we confront emerging challenges in the field of communicable diseases, it becomes increasingly clear that a multidisciplinary approach and a commitment to equity and justice are paramount.

Whether you are a student, researcher, healthcare professional, or simply an inquisitive mind eager to understand the complexities of infectious diseases, "An Introduction to the Sciences of Communicable Diseases" offers a comprehensive resource to inform, inspire, and guide your exploration of this vital subject.

I extend my heartfelt gratitude to all those who contributed to this endeavor, and I hope that this book serves as a valuable tool in the ongoing quest to safeguard public health and build a healthier, more resilient world.

Warm regards,

Dr. Nitish Bhatia

Professor and Head

Department of Pharmacology

Faculty of Pharmacy

Vishwakarma University

Pune

12 June 2024

# Acknowledgements

I extend my sincerest gratitude to the esteemed faculty members and dedicated staff of Vishwakarma University whose unwavering support and expertise have been instrumental in the creation of this book. Their guidance, encouragement, and invaluable contributions have enriched every aspect of this project.

I am profoundly grateful for their commitment to excellence in education and research, which has inspired me throughout the journey of crafting this resource. Their passion for advancing knowledge and their tireless efforts in nurturing the next generation of scholars have left an indelible mark on this endeavor.

To the faculty members and staff of Vishwakarma University, I offer my heartfelt thanks for their dedication, wisdom, and unwavering belief in the power of education to transform lives and shape a better future for us all.

With deepest appreciation,
Dr. Nitish Bhatia

# CHAPTER ONE

# DEFINITION AND CLASSIFICATION OF COMMUNICABLE DISEASES

**Introduction**

Communicable diseases, also known as infectious diseases, are illnesses caused by microorganisms such as bacteria, viruses, fungi, and parasites. These diseases are characterized by their ability to spread from one individual to another, either directly or indirectly. The study of communicable diseases encompasses their origins, mechanisms of transmission, epidemiology, clinical manifestations, prevention, and control. This chapter provides a comprehensive overview of the definition, classification, and fundamental concepts related to communicable diseases, emphasizing their impact on public health.

**Definition of Communicable Diseases**

Communicable diseases are defined as illnesses caused by infectious agents or their toxic products that are transmissible from an infected individual, animal, or reservoir to a susceptible host. The transmission can occur through various mechanisms, including direct contact, respiratory droplets, vectors, fomites, and contaminated food or water. The key elements in the definition of communicable diseases include:

1. **Causative Agents**: These are the microorganisms responsible for the disease. They include bacteria, viruses, fungi, and parasites.
2. **Transmission**: The process by which the infectious agent spreads from one host to another.
3. **Host Susceptibility**: The susceptibility of the host to infection, influenced by factors such as immunity, genetics, age, and comorbidities.
4. **Clinical Manifestations**: The signs and symptoms produced by the infection, which can range from asymptomatic to severe and life-threatening.

Understanding these components is essential for the effective management and control of communicable diseases, as they form the basis for epidemiological surveillance, diagnosis, treatment, and prevention strategies.

**Classification of Communicable Diseases**

Communicable diseases can be classified based on various criteria, including the type of causative agent, mode of transmission, clinical presentation, and epidemiological characteristics. This section provides a detailed classification of communicable diseases, highlighting the diversity and complexity of these infections.

**Classification by Causative Agent**

1. **Bacterial Diseases**: These are caused by pathogenic bacteria. Examples include tuberculosis (Mycobacterium tuberculosis), cholera (Vibrio cholerae), and syphilis (Treponema pallidum).
2. **Viral Diseases**: These diseases are caused by viruses. Notable examples include influenza (Influenza virus), HIV/AIDS (Human Immunodeficiency Virus), and COVID-19 (SARS-CoV-2).
3. **Fungal Diseases**: These are infections caused by fungi. Examples include candidiasis (Candida spp.), aspergillosis (Aspergillus spp.), and cryptococcosis (Cryptococcus neoformans).
4. **Parasitic Diseases**: These are caused by parasites. They include malaria (Plasmodium spp.), schistosomiasis (Schistosoma spp.), and giardiasis (Giardia lamblia).
5. **Prion Diseases**: These are caused by prions, which are infectious protein particles. Examples include Creutzfeldt-Jakob disease and bovine spongiform encephalopathy (mad cow disease).

**Classification by Mode of Transmission**

1. **Direct Transmission**: The infectious agent is transmitted directly from an infected individual to a susceptible host without an intermediate object or organism. This can occur through physical contact, sexual contact, and droplet spread.

   - **Contact Transmission**: Includes skin-to-skin contact, kissing, and sexual intercourse. Examples include herpes simplex virus infections and gonorrhea.

- **Droplet Transmission**: Occurs when respiratory droplets containing pathogens are expelled from an infected person during coughing, sneezing, or talking and are inhaled by a susceptible host. Examples include influenza and tuberculosis.

2. **Indirect Transmission**: The infectious agent is transmitted from an infected individual to a susceptible host through an intermediate object, organism, or environmental medium.

- **Vector-Borne Transmission**: The infectious agent is transmitted by vectors such as mosquitoes, ticks, and fleas. Examples include malaria, dengue fever, and Lyme disease.
- **Vehicle-Borne Transmission**: Involves the transmission of pathogens through contaminated food, water, or inanimate objects (fomites). Examples include hepatitis A (contaminated food or water) and norovirus (contaminated surfaces).
- **Airborne Transmission**: Pathogens are carried in the air in droplet nuclei or dust particles and are inhaled by a susceptible host. Examples include measles and chickenpox.
- **Zoonotic Transmission**: Involves the transmission of infectious agents from animals to humans. Examples include rabies and brucellosis.

**Classification by Clinical Presentation**

1. **Acute Diseases**: These diseases have a rapid onset and a short course. Symptoms are often severe but resolve within a short period. Examples include acute gastroenteritis, influenza, and measles.
2. **Chronic Diseases**: These diseases have a prolonged course, often lasting for months or years. Symptoms may be less severe but persist over time. Examples include tuberculosis, HIV/AIDS, and chronic hepatitis B.
3. **Latent Diseases**: These infections are characterized by periods of dormancy where the pathogen remains inactive in the host but can reactivate under certain conditions. Examples include herpes simplex virus infections and latent tuberculosis.
4. **Subclinical or Asymptomatic Diseases**: These infections do not produce noticeable symptoms in the host but can still be transmitted to others. Examples include asymptomatic carriers of Salmonella typhi and hepatitis B.

## Classification by Epidemiological Characteristics

1. **Endemic Diseases**: These diseases are consistently present in a specific geographic area or population. The number of cases remains relatively stable over time. Examples include malaria in certain parts of Africa and dengue fever in tropical regions.
2. **Epidemic Diseases**: These diseases occur at a higher than normal rate in a specific geographic area or population over a short period. Examples include the Ebola virus outbreaks and seasonal influenza epidemics.
3. **Pandemic Diseases**: These are epidemics that spread across multiple countries or continents, affecting a large

number of people. Examples include the 1918 influenza pandemic, the HIV/AIDS pandemic, and the COVID-19 pandemic.

4. **Sporadic Diseases**: These diseases occur infrequently and irregularly. Examples include cases of tetanus and rabies.

## Classification by Organ System Affected

1. **Respiratory Diseases**: These affect the respiratory system, including the upper and lower respiratory tracts. Examples include influenza, tuberculosis, and COVID-19.
2. **Gastrointestinal Diseases**: These affect the gastrointestinal tract, including the stomach and intestines. Examples include cholera, salmonellosis, and rotavirus infection.
3. **Cardiovascular Diseases**: These affect the heart and blood vessels. Examples include endocarditis and rheumatic fever.
4. **Neurological Diseases**: These affect the nervous system, including the brain and spinal cord. Examples include meningitis, encephalitis, and rabies.
5. **Dermatological Diseases**: These affect the skin and mucous membranes. Examples include impetigo, scabies, and cutaneous leishmaniasis.
6. **Genitourinary Diseases**: These affect the genital and urinary systems. Examples include gonorrhea, chlamydia, and urinary tract infections.

## Classification by Population at Risk

1. **Pediatric Diseases**: These primarily affect children. Examples include chickenpox, whooping cough, and hand-foot-and-mouth disease.
2. **Geriatric Diseases**: These primarily affect the elderly. Examples include shingles (herpes zoster) and respiratory syncytial virus (RSV) infection in older adults.
3. **Immunocompromised Diseases**: These affect individuals with weakened immune systems, such as those with HIV/AIDS, undergoing chemotherapy, or receiving organ transplants. Examples include opportunistic infections like Pneumocystis pneumonia and cytomegalovirus infection.
4. **Nosocomial or Healthcare-Associated Infections (HAIs)**: These infections are acquired in healthcare settings. Examples include methicillin-resistant Staphylococcus aureus (MRSA) and Clostridioides difficile infection.

**Key Concepts in the Study of Communicable Diseases**
Understanding communicable diseases requires familiarity with several key concepts that underpin their epidemiology, transmission, and control.

**Chain of Infection**
The chain of infection describes the sequence of events that allow the transmission of infectious agents from one host to another. Breaking any link in this chain can prevent the spread of disease. The chain of infection includes the following components:

1. **Infectious Agent**: The microorganism responsible for the disease (e.g., bacteria, virus, fungus, parasite).

2. **Reservoir**: The natural habitat where the infectious agent lives and multiplies (e.g., humans, animals, environment).
3. **Portal of Exit**: The pathway through which the infectious agent leaves the reservoir (e.g., respiratory secretions, feces, blood).
4. **Mode of Transmission**: The mechanism by which the infectious agent is transferred to a susceptible host (e.g., direct contact, vector-borne, airborne).
5. **Portal of Entry**: The pathway through which the infectious agent enters the susceptible host (e.g., mucous membranes, skin, respiratory tract).
6. **Susceptible Host**: An individual who is at risk of infection due to lack of immunity, underlying health conditions, or other factors.

## Infectious Dose and Pathogenicity

1. **Infectious Dose**: The quantity of an infectious agent required to establish an infection in a host. Lower infectious doses indicate higher infectivity.
2. **Pathogenicity**: The ability of an infectious agent to cause disease in a host. Pathogenicity is influenced by the agent's virulence factors, such as toxins, adhesion molecules, and immune evasion mechanisms.

## Incubation Period and Period of Infectivity

1. **Incubation Period**: The time interval between exposure to the infectious agent and the appearance of the first symptoms. Incubation periods can vary widely among different diseases.

2. **Period of Infectivity**: The time during which an infected individual can transmit the infectious agent to others. This period can overlap with, or occur before or after, the symptomatic phase.

### Herd Immunity

Herd immunity refers to the indirect protection from an infectious disease that occurs when a significant portion of a population becomes immune, either through vaccination or previous infection. This reduces the likelihood of disease transmission and provides protection to individuals who are not immune. Herd immunity thresholds vary depending on the infectious agent and its basic reproduction number (R0).

### Surveillance and Control Measures

Effective control of communicable diseases relies on robust surveillance systems and a range of public health interventions. Key control measures include:

1. **Vaccination**: Immunization programs aim to induce immunity and prevent the spread of vaccine-preventable diseases.
2. **Isolation and Quarantine**: Isolation separates infected individuals from healthy individuals, while quarantine restricts the movement of individuals who may have been exposed to an infectious agent.
3. **Vector Control**: Measures such as insecticide use, environmental management, and bed nets aim to reduce vector populations and interrupt transmission of vector-borne diseases.
4. **Sanitation and Hygiene**: Improvements in water quality, sanitation, and personal hygiene reduce the risk of transmission of waterborne and foodborne diseases.

5. **Antimicrobial Therapy**: The use of antibiotics, antivirals, antifungals, and antiparasitics to treat infections and reduce transmission.

### Emerging and Re-emerging Infectious Diseases

The landscape of communicable diseases is constantly evolving, with new pathogens emerging and previously controlled diseases re-emerging. Factors contributing to the emergence and re-emergence of infectious diseases include:

1. **Globalization and Travel**: Increased movement of people and goods facilitates the spread of infectious agents across borders.
2. **Urbanization**: Rapid urbanization can lead to overcrowded living conditions, inadequate sanitation, and increased contact between humans and animals, creating opportunities for disease transmission.
3. **Environmental Changes**: Climate change, deforestation, and changes in land use can alter the habitats of vectors and reservoirs, leading to the spread of infectious diseases.
4. **Antimicrobial Resistance**: The misuse and overuse of antimicrobial agents contribute to the development of resistant strains, making infections harder to treat and control.
5. **Public Health Infrastructure**: Weak healthcare systems, lack of surveillance, and inadequate response capacities can hinder the effective management of infectious disease outbreaks.

Communicable diseases represent a significant burden on global health, requiring a comprehensive understanding of their definition, classification, and underlying concepts. This chapter has provided an extensive overview of communicable diseases, emphasizing the diversity of infectious agents, modes of transmission, clinical presentations, and epidemiological characteristics. By understanding the fundamental principles of communicable diseases, public health professionals, clinicians, and researchers can develop and implement effective strategies for prevention, control, and treatment, ultimately reducing the impact of these diseases on individuals and communities worldwide.

# CHAPTER TWO

# HISTORICAL PERSPECTIVE AND MAJOR PANDEMICS

**Introduction**

The history of communicable diseases is intertwined with the history of humanity itself. Infectious diseases have shaped societies, influenced economic development, and altered the course of history. Major pandemics have led to profound social, political, and cultural changes. This chapter provides a comprehensive historical perspective on communicable diseases, examining major pandemics from antiquity to the present day. It highlights the epidemiological patterns, societal impacts, and advancements in medical science and public health that have emerged from these experiences.

**Ancient Pandemics**

**The Plague of Athens (430-426 BCE)**

One of the earliest recorded pandemics, the Plague of Athens, struck the city-state of Athens during the second year of the Peloponnesian War. Thucydides, an ancient historian and an eyewitness, documented the epidemic in detail. The causative agent of this plague remains a matter of debate among historians and scientists, with possible culprits including typhus, smallpox, and measles.

**Epidemiological Characteristics**

- **Spread**: The plague spread rapidly through the densely populated city of Athens, exacerbated by the crowded conditions caused by the influx of refugees.
- **Symptoms**: Descriptions include fever, redness and inflammation of the eyes, throat ulcers, and gastrointestinal symptoms.
- **Mortality**: The plague had a high mortality rate, with estimates suggesting that up to one-third of the population perished.

**Societal Impact**

The plague significantly weakened Athens, contributing to its eventual defeat by Sparta. The social fabric of Athenian society was disrupted, leading to lawlessness and moral decay as traditional norms broke down under the strain of the epidemic.

**The Antonine Plague (165-180 CE)**

The Antonine Plague, also known as the Plague of Galen, affected the Roman Empire during the reign of Emperor Marcus Aurelius. The exact pathogen responsible for this pandemic is believed to be either smallpox or measles, based on historical descriptions and modern analyses.

**Epidemiological Characteristics**

- **Spread**: The plague spread along the trade routes and through the Roman army, affecting large parts of the empire.
- **Symptoms**: Recorded symptoms included fever, diarrhea, and skin eruptions.
- **Mortality**: The plague caused significant mortality, with estimates suggesting that up to 5 million people died, including Emperor Lucius Verus.

### Societal Impact

The Antonine Plague severely impacted the Roman military, economic, and social structures. The loss of manpower weakened the Roman legions, while the economic burden of the pandemic strained the empire's resources. The psychological impact of the plague contributed to a sense of decline and vulnerability within the Roman Empire.

### Medieval Pandemics

### The Justinian Plague (541-542 CE)

The Justinian Plague, named after the Byzantine Emperor Justinian I, was the first recorded outbreak of bubonic plague caused by Yersinia pestis. It marked the beginning of the first plague pandemic, which recurred in waves over the next two centuries.

### Epidemiological Characteristics

- **Spread**: The plague spread from the port of Pelusium in Egypt to Constantinople and throughout the Byzantine Empire, facilitated by trade and military movements.
- **Symptoms**: Symptoms included fever, chills, swollen lymph nodes (buboes), and septicemia.
- **Mortality**: The mortality rate was extremely high, with contemporary accounts suggesting that millions died,

though exact figures are difficult to ascertain.

**Societal Impact**

The Justinian Plague had profound effects on the Byzantine Empire. It decimated the population, leading to labor shortages and economic decline. The reduced tax base weakened the empire's military capabilities, contributing to territorial losses and the eventual decline of the Byzantine state.

**The Black Death (1347-1351)**

The Black Death, the most infamous pandemic in history, swept through Europe, Asia, and North Africa in the mid-14th century. Caused by Yersinia pestis, this pandemic had devastating effects on the population and fundamentally altered the course of European history.

**Epidemiological Characteristics**

- **Spread**: The plague arrived in Europe via trading ships from the Black Sea, spreading rapidly through ports and along trade routes.
- **Symptoms**: Classic symptoms included buboes, fever, chills, vomiting, diarrhea, and delirium.
- **Mortality**: The Black Death killed an estimated 75-200 million people, reducing the world's population by a significant percentage.

**Societal Impact**

The Black Death had far-reaching consequences:

- **Demographic Changes**: The massive death toll led to severe labor shortages, which in turn led to increased wages and improved living conditions for peasants and workers.

- **Economic Shifts**: The reduction in population caused a decline in agricultural output and trade, while also leading to a redistribution of wealth.
- **Social Upheaval**: The plague weakened feudal structures, contributing to social mobility and eventually to the end of the feudal system in Europe.
- **Cultural Impact**: The Black Death profoundly influenced art, literature, and religious practices, fostering a preoccupation with death and the afterlife.

**Early Modern Pandemics**
**The Third Cholera Pandemic (1852-1860)**
Cholera, caused by the bacterium Vibrio cholerae, is an acute diarrheal disease that has caused multiple pandemics since the early 19th century. The third cholera pandemic was the most deadly, affecting Europe, Asia, and North America.

**Epidemiological Characteristics**

- **Spread**: Originating in India, the pandemic spread along trade routes to Europe and North America.
- **Symptoms**: Severe diarrhea, vomiting, and dehydration were hallmark symptoms.
- **Mortality**: Cholera had a high case fatality rate, particularly in areas with poor sanitation.

**Societal Impact**

- **Public Health Advances**: The devastation caused by cholera prompted significant public health reforms, including improvements in water and sanitation systems.

- **Epidemiological Discoveries:** The pandemic contributed to major advances in epidemiology, most notably John Snow's investigation of the 1854 London cholera outbreak, which demonstrated the role of contaminated water in disease transmission.

## The Spanish Flu (1918-1919)

The Spanish Flu pandemic, caused by the H1N1 influenza A virus, was one of the deadliest pandemics in history, occurring in the final year of World War I.

### Epidemiological Characteristics

- **Spread:** The virus spread globally, facilitated by troop movements and global transportation networks.
- **Symptoms:** Symptoms included fever, chills, muscle aches, and severe respiratory distress.
- **Mortality:** The Spanish Flu killed an estimated 50-100 million people worldwide, with a high mortality rate among young adults.

### Societal Impact

- **Healthcare Strain:** The rapid spread and high mortality of the virus overwhelmed healthcare systems and caused significant disruptions to daily life.
- **Public Health Measures:** The pandemic led to the implementation of various public health measures, including quarantine, isolation, and the use of masks, which remain fundamental strategies in controlling respiratory pandemics.
- **Scientific Advances:** The Spanish Flu spurred research into influenza viruses and the development of vaccines and antiviral treatments.

## Modern Pandemics

### The HIV/AIDS Pandemic (1981-Present)

HIV/AIDS, caused by the human immunodeficiency virus (HIV), emerged in the late 20th century and continues to be a significant global public health challenge.

### Epidemiological Characteristics

- **Spread**: HIV is transmitted through blood, sexual contact, and from mother to child during childbirth or breastfeeding.
- **Symptoms**: HIV infection progresses through stages, from acute infection to chronic asymptomatic phase, and eventually to AIDS, characterized by severe immunodeficiency.
- **Mortality**: Without treatment, HIV/AIDS is fatal, but antiretroviral therapy (ART) has dramatically improved survival rates.

### Societal Impact

- **Stigma and Discrimination**: HIV/AIDS has been associated with significant stigma and discrimination, affecting social and economic opportunities for those infected.
- **Healthcare Advances**: The epidemic has led to major advances in virology, immunology, and the development of ART, transforming HIV from a fatal disease to a manageable chronic condition.
- **Global Response**: International efforts, including the establishment of the Joint United Nations Programme on HIV/AIDS (UNAIDS), have been crucial in coordinating the global response to the epidemic.

### The H1N1 Influenza Pandemic (2009)

The H1N1 influenza pandemic of 2009, also known as the swine flu pandemic, was caused by a novel strain of H1N1 influenza A virus.

### Epidemiological Characteristics

- **Spread**: The virus spread rapidly worldwide, with the World Health Organization (WHO) declaring it a pandemic in June 2009.
- **Symptoms**: Symptoms were similar to seasonal influenza, including fever, cough, sore throat, and muscle aches.
- **Mortality**: The pandemic had a lower mortality rate compared to previous influenza pandemics, but it affected younger populations more severely.

### Societal Impact

- **Vaccine Development**: The rapid development and distribution of an H1N1 vaccine highlighted the importance of global cooperation in pandemic preparedness.
- **Public Health Response**: The pandemic underscored the need for effective surveillance systems, stockpiling of antiviral drugs, and public health communication strategies.

### The COVID-19 Pandemic (2019-Present)

The COVID-19 pandemic, caused by the novel coronavirus SARS-CoV-2, has had an unprecedented impact on global health and economies.

### Epidemiological Characteristics

- **Spread**: The virus spread globally from its initial outbreak in Wuhan, China, leading to widespread transmission and multiple waves of infection.
- **Symptoms**: Symptoms range from mild respiratory illness to severe pneumonia, acute respiratory distress syndrome (ARDS), and multi-organ failure.
- **Mortality**: COVID-19 has caused millions of deaths worldwide, with significant morbidity and long-term health effects in survivors.

## Societal Impact

- **Healthcare Systems**: The pandemic has strained healthcare systems, highlighting vulnerabilities and the need for robust healthcare infrastructure.
- **Economic Impact**: Lockdowns, travel restrictions, and other public health measures have led to significant economic disruption, affecting businesses and employment.
- **Vaccine Development**: The rapid development, approval, and distribution of COVID-19 vaccines have been unprecedented, demonstrating the potential for scientific innovation in response to global health crises.
- **Global Cooperation**: The pandemic has emphasized the importance of international cooperation in addressing global health threats and has led to the establishment of initiatives like COVAX to ensure equitable access to vaccines.

The history of communicable diseases is a testament to the profound impact that infectious agents have had on human societies throughout the ages. Major pandemics have not only caused immense mortality and morbidity but have also driven advancements in medical science, public health, and social organization. Understanding the historical perspective of communicable diseases and major pandemics provides valuable insights into the complex interplay between humans and pathogens, informing current and future efforts to prevent and control infectious diseases. As we continue to face emerging and re-emerging infectious threats, the lessons learned from past pandemics remain crucial in guiding our responses and safeguarding global health.

# CHAPTER THREE

# Importance of Studying Communicable Diseases in Public Health

**Introduction**

Communicable diseases have been a major public health challenge throughout human history. Their study is crucial for understanding, preventing, and managing diseases that can spread rapidly within populations, causing significant morbidity and mortality. This chapter delves into the multifaceted importance of studying communicable diseases in the field of public health. It explores their epidemiology, impact on health systems, economic and social consequences, and the development of policies and interventions to mitigate their effects.

**Epidemiological Significance**
**Understanding Disease Dynamics**

Studying communicable diseases involves comprehending the complex interactions between infectious agents, hosts, and the environment. This understanding is fundamental for predicting and controlling disease outbreaks.

**Transmission Dynamics**

- **Modes of Transmission**: Diseases can spread through various routes, including direct contact, airborne transmission, vector-borne pathways, and contaminated food or water. Recognizing these modes is essential for developing targeted control measures.
- **R0 (Basic Reproduction Number)**: This metric indicates the average number of secondary cases generated by one infected individual in a susceptible population. A disease with an R0 greater than 1 can lead to an outbreak, necessitating public health interventions to reduce transmission.

**Surveillance and Monitoring**

Effective disease surveillance systems are critical for early detection and response to infectious disease threats. Surveillance involves the systematic collection, analysis, and interpretation of health data.

- **Sentinel Surveillance**: Monitoring specific populations or locations to detect trends and emerging threats.
- **Syndromic Surveillance**: Using health-related data that precede diagnosis to signal a possible outbreak.
- **Molecular Surveillance**: Utilizing genetic sequencing to track pathogen evolution and spread.

**Outbreak Investigation and Control**

Prompt investigation of outbreaks is crucial to identify sources, modes of transmission, and implement control measures.

- **Epidemiological Investigations**: Involve case finding, contact tracing, and determining the index case (patient zero).
- **Intervention Strategies**: Include isolation and quarantine, vaccination, antimicrobial treatment, and public health communication to inform and educate the public.

## Impact on Health Systems
### Strain on Healthcare Infrastructure

Communicable diseases can overwhelm healthcare systems, especially during large-scale outbreaks or pandemics.

- **Hospitalization Rates**: High numbers of infected individuals requiring hospitalization can strain resources, leading to bed shortages and overburdened medical staff.
- **Healthcare Worker Safety**: Ensuring the safety of healthcare workers through adequate personal protective equipment (PPE) and infection control protocols is essential to maintain workforce capacity.

### Resource Allocation and Management

Effective management of resources, including medical supplies, vaccines, and medications, is vital during outbreaks.

- **Stockpiling**: Pre-positioning essential supplies to ensure rapid deployment during emergencies.
- **Supply Chain Management**: Ensuring the continuity and integrity of supply chains to prevent shortages and ensure timely distribution of medical supplies and equipment.

## Innovation and Capacity Building

Studying communicable diseases drives innovation in medical research and public health practices.

- **Vaccine Development**: Research into pathogen biology and immunology leads to the development of vaccines, which are crucial for preventing infectious diseases.
- **Diagnostic Tools**: Advances in diagnostic technologies enable rapid and accurate detection of pathogens, facilitating timely treatment and control measures.
- **Training and Education**: Building capacity through training healthcare professionals and public health workers ensures preparedness and effective response to infectious disease threats.

## Economic and Social Consequences

### Economic Burden

Communicable diseases impose significant economic costs on individuals, healthcare systems, and society as a whole.

- **Direct Costs**: Include medical expenses for treatment, hospitalization, and ongoing care for chronic conditions resulting from infections.
- **Indirect Costs**: Loss of productivity due to illness, long-term disability, or premature death, as well as the impact

on economic activities and trade.

## Case Study: COVID-19 Pandemic

The COVID-19 pandemic has illustrated the profound economic impact of a global health crisis.

- **Global GDP Impact**: The pandemic caused unprecedented economic disruptions, with global GDP contracting significantly in 2020 due to lockdowns, travel restrictions, and reduced consumer spending.
- **Government Expenditure**: Increased spending on healthcare infrastructure, social protection measures, and economic stimulus packages to mitigate the impact of the pandemic.

## Social Disruption

Infectious diseases can disrupt social structures, leading to widespread societal consequences.

- **Education**: School closures during outbreaks, such as during the COVID-19 pandemic, disrupted education for millions of children, potentially affecting their long-term development.
- **Social Inequality**: Vulnerable populations, including low-income communities and minorities, often bear a disproportionate burden of communicable diseases, exacerbating existing social inequalities.
- **Mental Health**: The psychological impact of infectious disease outbreaks, including fear, anxiety, and social isolation, can have long-lasting effects on mental health.

## Policy and Intervention Development
### Evidence-Based Public Health Policies

Studying communicable diseases provides the evidence base for developing effective public health policies and interventions.

**Vaccination Programs**

- **Immunization Strategies**: Developing and implementing vaccination schedules to achieve herd immunity and prevent disease outbreaks.
- **Global Initiatives**: Programs such as the Global Polio Eradication Initiative (GPEI) and the Expanded Programme on Immunization (EPI) aim to control and eliminate vaccine-preventable diseases worldwide.

**Antimicrobial Stewardship**

- **Rational Use of Antibiotics**: Promoting the judicious use of antibiotics to combat antimicrobial resistance (AMR), a major public health threat.
- **Surveillance of AMR**: Monitoring resistance patterns to inform treatment guidelines and policy decisions.

**Public Health Interventions**

Effective public health interventions are essential to control and prevent the spread of communicable diseases.

**Behavioral Interventions**

- **Health Education**: Educating the public about hygiene practices, safe food handling, and the importance of vaccination.
- **Behavior Change Communication (BCC)**: Using targeted communication strategies to promote healthy behaviors and reduce risky practices.

## Environmental Interventions

- **Sanitation and Hygiene**: Improving access to clean water, sanitation facilities, and promoting handwashing to reduce the spread of waterborne and hygiene-related diseases.
- **Vector Control**: Implementing measures to control vectors such as mosquitoes and ticks, which transmit diseases like malaria, dengue, and Lyme disease.

## Global Health Security

The interconnectedness of the modern world means that infectious disease threats can spread rapidly across borders, necessitating a coordinated global response.

### International Health Regulations (IHR)

- **Legal Framework**: The IHR (2005) provide a legal framework for global health security, requiring countries to report public health emergencies of international concern (PHEIC) and to develop core capacities for surveillance and response.

### Global Health Organizations

- **World Health Organization (WHO)**: Plays a central role in coordinating global health responses, providing technical guidance, and supporting countries in building public health capacity.
- **Centers for Disease Control and Prevention (CDC)**: Provides expertise and support for disease control and prevention efforts globally.

### Research and Technological Advancements

## Pathogen Research

Studying the biology and ecology of pathogens is crucial for developing effective interventions.

### Genomic Studies

- **Pathogen Genomics**: Sequencing the genomes of infectious agents to understand their evolution, transmission dynamics, and resistance mechanisms.
- **Metagenomics**: Studying microbial communities in various environments to identify potential pathogens and understand their interactions with hosts.

### Host-Pathogen Interactions

- **Immune Response**: Investigating how pathogens evade the immune system and how the body mounts an immune response, guiding vaccine and therapeutic development.
- **Pathogenesis**: Understanding the mechanisms by which pathogens cause disease, informing the development of targeted treatments and interventions.

### Technological Innovations

Advancements in technology play a critical role in the study and control of communicable diseases.

### Diagnostic Technologies

- **Rapid Diagnostic Tests (RDTs)**: Developing point-of-care tests that provide quick and accurate results, enabling timely treatment and control measures.
- **Molecular Diagnostics**: Techniques such as polymerase chain reaction (PCR) and next-generation sequencing (NGS) allow for precise identification and

characterization of pathogens.

## Digital Health

- **Surveillance Systems**: Leveraging digital technologies for real-time disease surveillance and data collection, enhancing the ability to detect and respond to outbreaks.
- **Telemedicine**: Expanding access to healthcare through telemedicine, particularly in remote or underserved areas, ensuring continuity of care during outbreaks.

## Ethical and Social Considerations
### Equity in Health
Ensuring equitable access to healthcare and interventions is a fundamental aspect of public health.
### Addressing Health Disparities

- **Social Determinants of Health**: Recognizing and addressing factors such as poverty, education, and access to healthcare that contribute to health disparities.
- **Inclusive Policies**: Developing policies that prioritize vulnerable populations and ensure equitable access to prevention and treatment services.

### Ethical Decision-Making
Ethical considerations are paramount in the study and management of communicable diseases.
### Research Ethics

- **Informed Consent**: Ensuring that participants in research studies understand the risks and benefits and provide informed consent.

- **Ethical Trials**: Conducting clinical trials in an ethical manner, with oversight to protect participants and ensure scientific integrity.

**Public Health Ethics**

- **Balancing Rights and Public Safety**: Implementing public health measures that protect the population while respecting individual rights and freedoms.
- **Transparency and Trust**: Maintaining transparency in communication and decision-making to build public trust and compliance with public health measures.

The study of communicable diseases is indispensable for public health. It provides the foundation for understanding disease dynamics, informing policy decisions, and developing effective interventions to prevent and control infectious diseases. The impact of communicable diseases on health systems, economies, and societies underscores the need for ongoing research, surveillance, and global cooperation. By addressing ethical and social considerations and leveraging technological advancements, public health professionals can better protect populations and improve health outcomes worldwide.

# CHAPTER FOUR

# BASICS OF MICROBIOLOGY

**Introduction**

Microbiology is the scientific study of microorganisms, a diverse group of microscopic entities that include bacteria, viruses, fungi, protozoa, and algae. This field is fundamental to our understanding of life on Earth, as microorganisms play crucial roles in ecological systems, human health, and biotechnology. This chapter delves into the basics of microbiology, covering the history, classification, structure, metabolism, genetics, and applications of microorganisms.

## Historical Background

### Early Observations and Discoveries

The origins of microbiology can be traced back to the invention of the microscope in the 17$^{\text{th}}$ century.

### Antonie van Leeuwenhoek

Antonie van Leeuwenhoek (1632-1723) is often referred to as the "Father of Microbiology." Using handcrafted microscopes, he was the first to observe and describe microorganisms, which he called "animalcules," in various samples, including pond water, saliva, and feces.

### Robert Hooke

Robert Hooke (1635-1703) was another pioneer who improved the design of early microscopes and provided detailed descriptions of microscopic structures in his book "Micrographia." He coined the term "cell" after observing the cell walls in cork tissue.

### Germ Theory of Disease

The 19th century saw significant advancements in understanding the role of microorganisms in disease.

### Louis Pasteur

Louis Pasteur (1822-1895) conducted experiments that refuted the theory of spontaneous generation and demonstrated that microorganisms cause fermentation and spoilage. He developed pasteurization to prevent the spoilage of wine and milk and created vaccines for rabies and anthrax.

### Robert Koch

Robert Koch (1843-1910) established the germ theory of disease by identifying the causative agents of tuberculosis, cholera, and anthrax. He formulated Koch's postulates, a set of criteria to establish a causal relationship between a microorganism and a disease.

### Classification of Microorganisms

Microorganisms are classified into various groups based on their characteristics. The major groups include bacteria, archaea, viruses, fungi, protozoa, and algae.

### Bacteria

### Characteristics

Bacteria are unicellular prokaryotes with a simple cell structure lacking a nucleus and membrane-bound organelles. They have a diverse range of shapes, including cocci (spherical), bacilli (rod-shaped), and spirilla (spiral).

### Classification

- **Gram Staining**: Bacteria are classified based on their cell wall composition as Gram-positive or Gram-negative, determined by the Gram stain technique.
- **Metabolism**: Bacteria can be classified as autotrophic (self-nourishing) or heterotrophic (dependent on external organic sources).
- **Oxygen Requirements**: They are categorized as aerobic, anaerobic, or facultative anaerobes based on their oxygen requirements.

## Archaea
### Characteristics

Archaea are unicellular prokaryotes similar in size and shape to bacteria but differ significantly in their genetic and biochemical properties. They often inhabit extreme environments, such as hot springs, salt lakes, and deep-sea hydrothermal vents.

### Classification

- **Methanogens**: Produce methane as a metabolic byproduct.
- **Halophiles**: Thrive in high-salt environments.
- **Thermophiles**: Live in extremely hot environments.

## Viruses
### Characteristics

Viruses are acellular entities consisting of a nucleic acid core (DNA or RNA) enclosed in a protein coat called a capsid. Some viruses also have a lipid envelope. They are obligate intracellular parasites, requiring a host cell to replicate.

### Classification

- **Genetic Material**: DNA viruses or RNA viruses.
- **Capsid Shape**: Icosahedral, helical, or complex.
- **Host Range**: Specific to certain hosts, such as bacteria (bacteriophages), plants, or animals.

## Fungi
### Characteristics

Fungi are eukaryotic organisms that can be unicellular (yeasts) or multicellular (molds and mushrooms). They have a complex cellular structure with a nucleus and membrane-bound organelles.

### Classification

- **Yeasts**: Unicellular fungi that reproduce by budding or binary fission.
- **Molds**: Multicellular fungi with a filamentous structure called hyphae.
- **Mushrooms**: Fruiting bodies of certain fungi that produce spores.

## Protozoa
### Characteristics

Protozoa are unicellular eukaryotes that exhibit diverse morphologies and modes of locomotion, including pseudopodia, cilia, and flagella. They are often free-living but can also be parasitic.

### Classification

- **Amoeboids**: Move using pseudopodia (e.g., Amoeba).
- **Ciliates**: Use cilia for movement (e.g., Paramecium).
- **Flagellates**: Move using flagella (e.g., Trypanosoma).
- **Sporozoans**: Non-motile and often parasitic (e.g., Plasmodium).

## Algae

### Characteristics

Algae are photosynthetic eukaryotes that can be unicellular or multicellular. They play a crucial role in aquatic ecosystems by producing oxygen and serving as the base of the food web.

### Classification

- **Green Algae**: Contain chlorophyll a and b (e.g., Chlamydomonas).
- **Red Algae**: Contain chlorophyll a and phycobiliproteins (e.g., Porphyra).
- **Brown Algae**: Contain chlorophyll a and c and fucoxanthin (e.g., kelp).

## Structure of Microorganisms

Understanding the structural components of microorganisms is essential for comprehending their functions and interactions with the environment.

### Bacterial Cell Structure

### Cell Wall

The bacterial cell wall provides structural support and shape and protects against osmotic pressure. It is composed of peptidoglycan, a polymer of sugars and amino acids.

- **Gram-Positive Bacteria**: Have a thick peptidoglycan layer and teichoic acids.
- **Gram-Negative Bacteria**: Have a thin peptidoglycan layer, an outer membrane containing lipopolysaccharides, and porins.

### Cell Membrane

The bacterial cell membrane is a phospholipid bilayer with embedded proteins that control the passage of substances in and out of the cell.

### Cytoplasm

The cytoplasm contains the cell's genetic material, ribosomes, and various inclusions. The nucleoid region houses the bacterial chromosome.

### Appendages

- **Flagella**: Long, whip-like structures used for motility.
- **Pili**: Short, hair-like structures used for attachment and conjugation (DNA transfer).

### Viral Structure

### Capsid

The capsid is a protein shell that encases the viral genome. It can be icosahedral, helical, or complex in shape.

### Envelope

Some viruses have a lipid envelope derived from the host cell membrane, which contains viral glycoproteins essential for host cell entry.

### Genome

Viral genomes can be composed of DNA or RNA, which can be single-stranded or double-stranded.

### Fungal Structure

### Cell Wall

Fungal cell walls are composed of chitin, glucans, and proteins, providing structural support and protection.

### Hyphae and Mycelium

Multicellular fungi form filamentous structures called hyphae, which collectively form a mycelium. Hyphae grow and branch to absorb nutrients from the environment.

### Spores

Fungi reproduce by producing spores, which can be sexual or asexual. Spores are dispersed to new environments to germinate and form new fungal colonies.

## Protozoan Structure

### Cell Membrane

Protozoa have a flexible cell membrane that allows for various shapes and movements.

### Organelles

Protozoa possess typical eukaryotic organelles, including a nucleus, mitochondria, and endoplasmic reticulum. Specialized structures like contractile vacuoles regulate osmotic pressure.

### Locomotion Structures

- **Pseudopodia**: Extensions of the cell membrane and cytoplasm used for movement and feeding.
- **Cilia**: Short, hair-like structures used for locomotion and feeding.
- **Flagella**: Long, whip-like structures used for movement.

## Algal Structure

### Cell Wall

Algal cell walls vary in composition, including cellulose, silica, and calcium carbonate, providing structural support and protection.

### Chloroplasts

Chloroplasts in algae contain photosynthetic pigments, including chlorophyll, carotenoids, and phycobiliproteins, enabling photosynthesis.

### Vacuoles

Algae often have large central vacuoles for storage and maintaining cell turgor.

## Metabolism of Microorganisms

Microorganisms exhibit diverse metabolic pathways to obtain energy and nutrients from their environment.

**Bacterial Metabolism**

**Autotrophy**

Autotrophic bacteria synthesize their own food from inorganic sources.

- **Photoautotrophs**: Use light energy to convert carbon dioxide and water into organic compounds (e.g., cyanobacteria).
- **Chemoautotrophs**: Use energy from chemical reactions involving inorganic compounds (e.g., nitrifying bacteria).

**Heterotrophy**

Heterotrophic bacteria rely on organic compounds for energy and carbon.

- **Photoheterotrophs**: Use light energy but obtain carbon from organic sources.
- **Chemoheterotrophs**: Obtain energy and carbon from organic compounds (e.g., Escherichia coli).

**Respiration and Fermentation**

- **Aerobic Respiration**: Complete oxidation of organic compounds to carbon dioxide and water using oxygen as the final electron acceptor.
- **Anaerobic Respiration**: Oxidation of organic compounds using inorganic molecules other than oxygen as electron acceptors (e.g., nitrate, sulfate).
- **Fermentation**: Partial oxidation of organic compounds to produce energy, typically resulting in the production

of organic acids, alcohols, and gases.

### Viral Metabolism

Viruses lack metabolic machinery and depend entirely on the host cell for replication. They hijack the host cell's metabolic pathways to synthesize viral components.

### Fungal Metabolism

### Saprophytic Nutrition

Most fungi are saprophytes, decomposing dead organic matter to obtain nutrients. They secrete extracellular enzymes to break down complex molecules into simpler forms that can be absorbed.

### Parasitic and Mutualistic Relationships

Some fungi are parasites, obtaining nutrients from living hosts, often causing disease. Others form mutualistic relationships, such as mycorrhizae with plants, where both organisms benefit.

### Protozoan Metabolism

Protozoa exhibit diverse metabolic pathways, including heterotrophy, autotrophy, and mixotrophy (combining both modes).

- **Phagocytosis**: Engulfing food particles or other cells.
- **Pinocytosis**: Engulfing liquid nutrient solutions.
- **Photosynthesis**: In photosynthetic protozoa, such as Euglena.

### Algal Metabolism

Algae primarily use photosynthesis to convert light energy into chemical energy, producing oxygen and organic compounds. Some algae can also absorb dissolved organic compounds.

### Genetics of Microorganisms

Microbial genetics is the study of how microorganisms inherit traits and how their genes are organized, expressed, and regulated.

## Bacterial Genetics

### Chromosomes and Plasmids

Bacteria typically have a single circular chromosome located in the nucleoid region. They also have plasmids, small circular DNA molecules that carry non-essential but beneficial genes.

### Gene Expression and Regulation

- **Operons**: Groups of genes regulated together by a single promoter and operator (e.g., lac operon).
- **Quorum Sensing**: A communication mechanism that regulates gene expression based on population density.

### Genetic Variation

- **Mutations**: Spontaneous or induced changes in the DNA sequence.
- **Horizontal Gene Transfer**: Exchange of genetic material between bacteria through transformation, transduction, and conjugation.

## Viral Genetics

### Genome Organization

Viral genomes can be linear or circular, single-stranded or double-stranded, and can vary greatly in size.

### Replication Strategies

- **DNA Viruses**: Replicate using host cell DNA polymerases.

- **RNA Viruses**: Replicate using viral RNA-dependent RNA polymerases.
- **Retroviruses**: Use reverse transcriptase to convert RNA into DNA, which integrates into the host genome (e.g., HIV).

### Fungal Genetics

### Chromosomes

Fungi have multiple linear chromosomes contained within a nucleus. Their genetic organization is similar to other eukaryotes.

### Reproduction

Fungi reproduce both sexually and asexually, with genetic recombination occurring during sexual reproduction, leading to increased genetic diversity.

### Protozoan Genetics

Protozoa exhibit typical eukaryotic genetic organization with linear chromosomes contained within a nucleus. They reproduce asexually through binary fission or multiple fission and sexually through conjugation or gametogenesis.

### Algal Genetics

Algae have genetic systems similar to other eukaryotes, with linear chromosomes in a nucleus. They can reproduce asexually through mitosis and sexually through the fusion of gametes.

### Applications of Microbiology

Microorganisms have numerous applications in various fields, including medicine, agriculture, industry, and environmental science.

### Medicine

### Antibiotics

Many antibiotics, such as penicillin, are derived from microorganisms. They are used to treat bacterial infections by inhibiting cell wall synthesis, protein synthesis, or other essential processes.

**Vaccines**

Vaccines are developed using live attenuated, inactivated, or subunit forms of pathogens to induce immunity against infectious diseases.

**Biotechnology**

Genetically engineered microorganisms produce pharmaceuticals, such as insulin, growth hormones, and monoclonal antibodies.

**Agriculture**

**Biocontrol Agents**

Microorganisms are used as biocontrol agents to manage agricultural pests and diseases, reducing the reliance on chemical pesticides.

**Biofertilizers**

Nitrogen-fixing bacteria, such as Rhizobium, and mycorrhizal fungi enhance soil fertility by increasing nutrient availability to plants.

**Industry**

**Fermentation**

Microorganisms are used in fermentation processes to produce a wide range of products, including alcohol, organic acids, and biofuels.

**Bioremediation**

Microorganisms degrade environmental pollutants, such as oil spills and toxic waste, through bioremediation processes, contributing to environmental cleanup.

**Environmental Science**

**Microbial Ecology**

Microorganisms play vital roles in nutrient cycling, decomposition, and maintaining ecological balance in various ecosystems.

**Climate Change**

Microbial processes, such as methanogenesis and denitrification, influence greenhouse gas emissions and global climate patterns.

The basics of microbiology encompass the study of microorganisms' diverse forms, structures, metabolic pathways, genetic mechanisms, and their vast applications. From the early discoveries of Antonie van Leeuwenhoek to modern biotechnological advancements, microbiology has profoundly impacted our understanding of life and the development of various fields. By continuing to explore and harness the potential of microorganisms, we can address critical challenges in health, agriculture, industry, and the environment, ultimately improving the quality of life on Earth.

# CHAPTER FIVE

# MICROBIAL DIVERSITY AND THEIR ECOLOGICAL ROLES

## Introduction

Microbial diversity encompasses the vast variety of microorganisms, including bacteria, archaea, viruses, fungi, protozoa, and algae, each exhibiting unique characteristics and performing essential ecological roles. Microorganisms are ubiquitous, inhabiting every conceivable environment on Earth, from extreme habitats like hot springs and deep-sea hydrothermal vents to more common environments such as soil, water, and the human body. Understanding microbial diversity and their ecological roles is crucial for comprehending ecosystem functioning, biogeochemical cycles, and the overall health of the planet.

**Types of Microorganisms and Their Diversity**

## Bacteria

### Characteristics and Diversity

Bacteria are unicellular prokaryotes with diverse shapes, sizes, and metabolic capabilities. They inhabit a wide range of environments and are essential for various ecological processes.

- **Morphological Diversity**: Bacteria come in various shapes, including cocci (spherical), bacilli (rod-shaped), spirilla (spiral), and filamentous forms.
- **Metabolic Diversity**: Bacteria exhibit diverse metabolic pathways, including photosynthesis, chemosynthesis, aerobic and anaerobic respiration, and fermentation.

### Ecological Roles

- **Decomposers**: Bacteria decompose organic matter, recycling nutrients back into the ecosystem.
- **Nitrogen Fixation**: Certain bacteria, such as Rhizobium, convert atmospheric nitrogen into ammonia, a form usable by plants.
- **Symbiosis**: Bacteria form symbiotic relationships with plants, animals, and other microorganisms, contributing to nutrient exchange, digestion, and disease resistance.

## Archaea

### Characteristics and Diversity

Archaea are unicellular prokaryotes that differ from bacteria in their genetic, biochemical, and structural properties. They often thrive in extreme environments but are also found in more moderate habitats.

- **Methanogens**: Produce methane as a metabolic byproduct.
- **Halophiles**: Thrive in high-salt environments.
- **Thermophiles**: Live in extremely hot environments.
- **Acidophiles**: Survive in highly acidic conditions.

**Ecological Roles**

- **Methanogenesis**: Methanogenic archaea play a crucial role in the carbon cycle by producing methane, a potent greenhouse gas.
- **Extreme Environments**: Archaea contribute to nutrient cycles and primary production in extreme environments where other life forms are scarce.

**Viruses**

**Characteristics and Diversity**

Viruses are acellular entities consisting of genetic material (DNA or RNA) enclosed in a protein coat. They are obligate intracellular parasites, requiring a host cell to replicate.

- **Genome Diversity**: Viral genomes vary greatly in size and complexity, from small RNA viruses to large DNA viruses.
- **Host Range**: Viruses infect all forms of life, including bacteria (bacteriophages), plants, animals, and other microorganisms.

**Ecological Roles**

- **Regulation of Microbial Populations**: Viruses control microbial populations through infection and lysis, influencing nutrient cycling and ecosystem dynamics.

- **Horizontal Gene Transfer**: Viruses facilitate the transfer of genes between organisms, contributing to genetic diversity and evolution.

## Fungi
### Characteristics and Diversity

Fungi are eukaryotic organisms that can be unicellular (yeasts) or multicellular (molds and mushrooms). They exhibit diverse morphologies and reproductive strategies.

- **Morphological Diversity**: Fungi have structures like hyphae, mycelium, and fruiting bodies.
- **Reproductive Diversity**: Fungi reproduce sexually and asexually through spores.

### Ecological Roles

- **Decomposers**: Fungi decompose complex organic matter, including lignin and cellulose, recycling nutrients into the ecosystem.
- **Symbiosis**: Fungi form mutualistic relationships, such as mycorrhizae with plant roots, enhancing nutrient uptake.
- **Pathogens**: Some fungi cause diseases in plants, animals, and humans, impacting ecological and economic systems.

## Protozoa
### Characteristics and Diversity

Protozoa are unicellular eukaryotes with diverse morphologies and modes of locomotion, including pseudopodia, cilia, and flagella. They inhabit various environments, from soil and water to the human body.

- **Morphological Diversity**: Protozoa exhibit various shapes and structures adapted to their ecological niches.
- **Locomotion Diversity**: Different groups of protozoa use distinct structures for movement and feeding.

## Ecological Roles

- **Predators**: Protozoa regulate microbial populations by preying on bacteria and other microorganisms.
- **Nutrient Cycling**: Through their feeding activities, protozoa contribute to nutrient cycling and the decomposition of organic matter.
- **Symbiosis**: Some protozoa form symbiotic relationships with other organisms, such as termites, aiding in digestion.

## Algae
### Characteristics and Diversity

Algae are photosynthetic eukaryotes that can be unicellular or multicellular. They play a crucial role in aquatic ecosystems as primary producers.

- **Morphological Diversity**: Algae range from microscopic phytoplankton to large seaweeds.
- **Pigment Diversity**: Algae contain various photosynthetic pigments, including chlorophylls, carotenoids, and phycobiliproteins.

## Ecological Roles

- **Primary Production**: Algae produce oxygen and organic compounds through photosynthesis, forming the base of aquatic food webs.
- **Habitat Formation**: Algae create habitats for other organisms, such as coral reefs formed by symbiotic algae.
- **Nutrient Cycling**: Algae contribute to nutrient cycling, including carbon and nitrogen fixation.

## Ecological Roles of Microorganisms

Microorganisms are integral to ecosystem functioning and stability. They perform essential ecological roles, including nutrient cycling, primary production, decomposition, and symbiosis.

### Nutrient Cycling

### Carbon Cycle

Microorganisms play a pivotal role in the carbon cycle by mediating the transformation and movement of carbon through the ecosystem.

- **Photosynthesis**: Algae and cyanobacteria fix carbon dioxide into organic matter through photosynthesis.
- **Decomposition**: Bacteria and fungi decompose organic matter, releasing carbon dioxide and methane into the atmosphere.
- **Methanogenesis**: Methanogenic archaea produce methane from organic substrates in anaerobic environments.
- **Methanotrophy**: Methanotrophic bacteria oxidize methane, converting it back to carbon dioxide.

### Nitrogen Cycle

Microorganisms are essential for the nitrogen cycle, converting nitrogen between its various chemical forms.

- **Nitrogen Fixation**: Nitrogen-fixing bacteria and archaea convert atmospheric nitrogen into ammonia, which plants can assimilate.
- **Nitrification**: Nitrifying bacteria oxidize ammonia to nitrite and then to nitrate.
- **Denitrification**: Denitrifying bacteria convert nitrate to nitrogen gas, returning it to the atmosphere.
- **Ammonification**: Decomposers convert organic nitrogen into ammonia during the decomposition of organic matter.

### Sulfur Cycle

Microorganisms mediate the sulfur cycle by transforming sulfur compounds through various metabolic processes.

- **Sulfate Reduction**: Sulfate-reducing bacteria convert sulfate to hydrogen sulfide in anaerobic conditions.
- **Sulfur Oxidation**: Sulfur-oxidizing bacteria convert hydrogen sulfide to sulfate in aerobic conditions.
- **Decomposition**: Fungi and bacteria decompose organic sulfur compounds, releasing hydrogen sulfide.

### Phosphorus Cycle

Microorganisms influence the phosphorus cycle by solubilizing and mineralizing phosphorus compounds.

- **Mineralization**: Decomposers break down organic phosphorus into inorganic forms usable by plants.

- **Solubilization**: Phosphate-solubilizing bacteria convert insoluble phosphorus compounds into soluble forms through the secretion of organic acids.

## Primary Production

Microorganisms, particularly algae and cyanobacteria, are primary producers that convert solar energy into chemical energy through photosynthesis. This process produces oxygen and organic compounds, forming the foundation of food webs in aquatic and terrestrial ecosystems.

- **Phytoplankton**: Microscopic algae and cyanobacteria are major primary producers in marine and freshwater ecosystems.
- **Biofilms**: Photosynthetic microorganisms form biofilms on surfaces, contributing to primary production in various environments.

## Decomposition

Decomposers, including bacteria and fungi, break down dead organic matter, recycling nutrients back into the ecosystem. This process is crucial for maintaining soil fertility and ecosystem productivity.

- **Litter Decomposition**: Fungi and bacteria decompose leaf litter and other plant debris, releasing nutrients into the soil.
- **Wood Decomposition**: Certain fungi, such as white-rot and brown-rot fungi, decompose lignin and cellulose in wood, contributing to nutrient cycling in forest ecosystems.

**Symbiosis**

Microorganisms form various symbiotic relationships with other organisms, including mutualism, commensalism, and parasitism.

**Mutualism**

In mutualistic relationships, both partners benefit from the interaction.

- **Mycorrhizae**: Fungi form mycorrhizal associations with plant roots, enhancing nutrient uptake and plant growth.
- **Rhizobia**: Nitrogen-fixing bacteria form nodules on the roots of leguminous plants, providing them with bioavailable nitrogen.
- **Lichens**: Symbiotic associations between fungi and photosynthetic algae or cyanobacteria, contributing to primary production and nutrient cycling.

**Commensalism**

In commensal relationships, one partner benefits while the other is unaffected.

- **Epiphytic Bacteria**: Bacteria living on the surfaces of plants without harming them, potentially providing benefits like nutrient acquisition.
- **Skin Microbiota**: Commensal bacteria on human skin protect against pathogenic microbes by occupying niches and producing antimicrobial compounds.

**Parasitism**

In parasitic relationships, one partner benefits at the expense of the other.

- **Pathogenic Bacteria**: Bacteria that cause diseases in plants, animals, and humans, impacting ecological and economic systems.
- **Fungal Pathogens**: Fungi that infect plants and animals, leading to diseases and ecosystem disruptions.

## Microbial Interactions in Ecosystems

Microorganisms interact with each other and with other organisms in complex ways, shaping ecosystem structure and function.

### Microbial Competition

Microorganisms compete for resources such as nutrients, space, and light. Competition can influence microbial community composition and ecosystem dynamics.

- **Antibiotic Production**: Some bacteria produce antibiotics to inhibit competitors, shaping microbial communities.
- **Resource Partitioning**: Microorganisms adapt to utilize different resources or occupy distinct niches to reduce competition.

### Microbial Cooperation

Microorganisms often cooperate through mutualistic interactions and communal living.

- **Biofilms**: Complex communities of microorganisms embedded in a matrix of extracellular polymeric substances, enhancing survival and function in various environments.
- **Syntrophy**: Cooperative interaction where one microorganism's metabolic byproducts are used as

substrates by another, facilitating nutrient cycling and energy production.

## Microbial Predation

Microorganisms can prey on each other, influencing population dynamics and community structure.

- **Protozoan Predation**: Protozoa feed on bacteria and other microorganisms, regulating microbial populations.
- **Bacteriophages**: Viruses that infect and lyse bacteria, controlling bacterial populations and facilitating horizontal gene transfer.

## Microbial Diversity in Extreme Environments

Microorganisms are capable of thriving in extreme environments, exhibiting remarkable adaptations that allow them to survive and function under harsh conditions.

### Extremophiles

Extremophiles are microorganisms that thrive in extreme environments, including high or low temperatures, high salinity, extreme pH, and high pressure.

### Thermophiles and Hyperthermophiles

Thermophiles and hyperthermophiles thrive in high-temperature environments, such as hot springs and hydrothermal vents.

- **Thermostable Enzymes**: These microorganisms produce enzymes that remain functional at high temperatures, useful in industrial applications.
- **Heat-Shock Proteins**: Proteins that help maintain cellular function and integrity under thermal stress.

### Psychrophiles

Psychrophiles thrive in cold environments, such as polar regions and deep ocean waters.

- **Cold-Active Enzymes**: Enzymes that remain functional at low temperatures, enabling metabolic processes.
- **Antifreeze Proteins**: Proteins that prevent ice crystal formation within cells.

### Halophiles

Halophiles thrive in high-salt environments, such as salt flats and saline lakes.

- **Osmoprotectants**: Molecules that help maintain osmotic balance in high-salt conditions.
- **Ion Pumps**: Proteins that regulate ion concentrations to prevent cellular damage.

### Acidophiles and Alkaliphiles

Acidophiles and alkaliphiles thrive in environments with extreme pH, such as acidic hot springs and alkaline lakes.

- **pH Homeostasis**: Mechanisms that maintain internal pH within a viable range despite external pH extremes.
- **Proton Pumps**: Proteins that regulate proton concentrations to maintain pH balance.

### Adaptations to Extreme Environments

Microorganisms exhibit various adaptations that allow them to survive and function in extreme environments.

- **Membrane Adaptations**: Alterations in membrane composition to maintain fluidity and integrity under extreme conditions.
- **DNA Repair Mechanisms**: Enhanced DNA repair systems to counteract damage caused by extreme environmental stressors.
- **Protective Pigments**: Pigments that protect against UV radiation and other environmental stressors.

## Microbial Diversity and Human Health

Microbial diversity significantly impacts human health, both positively and negatively. The human microbiome, the collection of microorganisms living on and within the human body, plays a crucial role in health and disease.

### Human Microbiome

The human microbiome consists of diverse microbial communities that inhabit various body sites, including the skin, mouth, gut, and respiratory tract.

### Gut Microbiome

The gut microbiome is one of the most diverse and complex microbial communities, essential for digestion, nutrient absorption, and immune function.

- **Digestion and Metabolism**: Gut microbes help digest complex carbohydrates and produce short-chain fatty acids, vitamins, and other metabolites.
- **Immune Regulation**: The gut microbiome interacts with the immune system, promoting immune tolerance and protecting against pathogens.
- **Disease Associations**: Dysbiosis, an imbalance in the gut microbiome, is associated with various diseases, including inflammatory bowel disease, obesity, and diabetes.

## Skin Microbiome

The skin microbiome protects against pathogenic microbes, modulates immune responses, and contributes to skin health.

- **Barrier Function**: Commensal bacteria on the skin prevent colonization by pathogens by competing for resources and producing antimicrobial compounds.
- **Immune Modulation**: Skin microbes interact with the immune system, influencing immune responses and inflammation.

## Pathogenic Microorganisms

Pathogenic microorganisms cause diseases in humans, impacting health and well-being.

### Bacterial Pathogens

Bacterial pathogens cause a wide range of infections, from minor skin infections to life-threatening diseases.

- **Antibiotic Resistance**: The emergence of antibiotic-resistant bacteria poses a significant public health challenge, necessitating new approaches to treatment and prevention.
- **Virulence Factors**: Bacterial pathogens produce virulence factors, such as toxins and enzymes, that enable them to infect and damage host tissues.

### Viral Pathogens

Viral pathogens cause diseases ranging from the common cold to severe illnesses like HIV/AIDS and COVID-19.

- **Vaccination**: Vaccines are essential for preventing viral infections and reducing their spread within populations.
- **Antiviral Therapies**: Antiviral drugs target specific stages of viral replication, offering treatment options for viral infections.

## Fungal Pathogens

Fungal pathogens cause infections, particularly in immunocompromised individuals.

- **Opportunistic Infections**: Fungi like Candida and Aspergillus cause opportunistic infections in individuals with weakened immune systems.
- **Antifungal Resistance**: The rise of antifungal-resistant strains necessitates the development of new antifungal therapies.

## Protozoan Pathogens

Protozoan pathogens cause diseases such as malaria, amoebiasis, and giardiasis.

- **Vector Control**: Controlling vectors, such as mosquitoes, is crucial for preventing the spread of protozoan diseases.
- **Antiprotozoal Drugs**: Antiprotozoal medications target specific stages of protozoan life cycles, offering treatment options for infections.

Microbial diversity encompasses the vast array of microorganisms inhabiting diverse environments and performing essential ecological roles. From nutrient cycling and primary production to decomposition and symbiosis, microorganisms are integral to ecosystem functioning and stability. Understanding microbial diversity and their ecological roles provides insights into ecosystem dynamics, human health, and potential applications in biotechnology, medicine, and environmental management. As research continues to uncover the complexities of microbial interactions and adaptations, the significance of microorganisms in shaping life on Earth becomes increasingly evident. Through continued exploration and appreciation of microbial diversity, we can harness their potential to address global challenges and enhance the quality of life on our planet.

# CHAPTER SIX

# IDENTIFICATION METHODS AND TOOLS USED IN MICROBIOLOGY

**1. Microscopic Techniques:**

- **Light Microscopy:**

  - **Gram Staining:** Classifies bacteria into Gram-positive and Gram-negative based on cell wall characteristics.
  - **Simple Staining:** Uses a single stain to enhance contrast and visualize cell morphology.

- **Fluorescence Microscopy:**

  - **Fluorescent Dyes:** Stains cells with fluorescent dyes, enabling the visualization of specific cellular structures. Useful for live-cell imaging.

## 2. Cultural Methods:

- **Culture Media:**

  - **Nutrient Agar:** Supports the growth of a wide range of microorganisms.
  - **Blood Agar:** Differentiates bacteria based on their ability to lyse red blood cells.
  - **Selective Media:** Inhibits the growth of unwanted microorganisms, allowing the isolation of specific species.

- **Colonial Morphology:**

  - **Size:** Reflects the growth rate of microorganisms.
  - **Color, Shape, Texture:** Provides visual clues about the microbial species.

## 3. Biochemical Tests:

- **API Strips (Analytical Profile Index):**

  - **Multiple Compartments:** Contain various biochemical tests, such as carbohydrate utilization and enzyme activity.
  - **Database Comparison:** Results are compared to databases for identification.

- **Bacterial Metabolism Tests:**

  - **Fermentation Tests:** Measure the ability of bacteria to ferment specific sugars.

- **Oxidase and Catalase Tests:** Assess enzymatic activities.

**4. Molecular Methods:**

- **Polymerase Chain Reaction (PCR):**

  - **Amplification:** Replicates specific DNA sequences.
  - **Applications:** Used in DNA fingerprinting, diagnostics, and gene cloning.

- **DNA Sequencing:**

  - **Sanger Sequencing:** Traditional method for determining DNA sequences.
  - **Next-Generation Sequencing (NGS):** Allows high-throughput sequencing of entire genomes.

- **16S rRNA Sequencing:**

  - **Universal Marker:** Targets the 16S ribosomal RNA gene for bacterial identification.
  - **Phylogenetic Analysis:** Used to study microbial diversity.

- **Whole Genome Sequencing (WGS):**

  - **Comprehensive Analysis:** Provides a complete genomic profile for accurate identification.
  - **Comparative Genomics:** Helps study genetic variations among strains.

**5. Immunological Methods:**

- **Enzyme-Linked Immunosorbent Assay (ELISA):**

  - **Antigen-Antibody Interaction:** Detects specific antigens or antibodies.
  - **Colorimetric or Fluorometric Detection:** Quantifies the binding reaction.

- **Western Blot:**

  - **Protein Detection:** Identifies specific proteins through antibody binding.
  - **Electrophoresis:** Separates proteins based on size.

6. **Serological Tests:**

- **Agglutination Tests:**

  - **Clumping Reaction:** Detects the presence of antibodies or antigens.
  - **Applications:** Blood typing, identification of bacterial strains.

- **Precipitation Tests:**

  - **Formation of Precipitate:** Indicates the presence of soluble antigens.
  - **Applications:** Identifying bacterial or viral infections.

7. **Mass Spectrometry:**

- **Matrix-Assisted Laser Desorption/Ionization Time-of-Flight Mass Spectrometry (MALDI-TOF MS):**

- **Protein Profiling:** Analyzes microbial proteins for identification.
- **Database Comparison:** Matches mass spectra for accurate identification.

**8. Flow Cytometry:**

- **Cell Sorting:**

  - **Automated Sorting:** Separates microbial cells based on size, shape, and fluorescence patterns.
  - **High Throughput:** Enables the analysis of large populations of cells.

**9. Genomic and Proteomic Approaches:**

- **Comparative Genomic Hybridization (CGH):**

  - **Genome Comparison:** Compares the genomic content of different strains.
  - **Identifying Genomic Variations:** Helps understand genetic diversity.

- **Proteomics:**

  - **Global Protein Analysis:** Studies the entire complement of proteins expressed by microorganisms.
  - **Functional Insights:** Provides information on protein functions and interactions.

**10. Phenotypic Tests:**

- **Antimicrobial Susceptibility Testing:**

  - **Determines Sensitivity:** Evaluates the response of microorganisms to antibiotics.
  - **Disk Diffusion, Broth Dilution:** Common methods for susceptibility testing.

- **Metabolic Pathway Analysis:**

  - **Substrate Utilization:** Examines the ability of microorganisms to metabolize specific substrates.
  - **Biolog Plates:** Utilized for metabolic profiling.

**11. Electron Microscopy:**

- **Transmission Electron Microscopy (TEM):**

  - **Ultrastructural Imaging:** Provides detailed images of microbial structures.
  - **High Magnification:** Allows visualization at the nanoscale.

**12. Automated Systems:**

- **Automated Microbiology Systems:**

  - **Robotics and Computerized Analysis:** Provide rapid identification of microorganisms.
  - **Integrated Software:** Assists in result interpretation.

**13. MALDI Biotyper:**

- **Extension of MALDI-TOF MS:**

- **Specifically Designed for Microbial Identification:** Matches mass spectra to a comprehensive database.
- **Rapid Identification:** Enables quick and accurate microbial identification.

## 14. Phage Typing:

- **Identifying Bacteria:**

  - **Phage Susceptibility Patterns:** Differentiates bacterial strains based on their susceptibility to bacteriophages.
  - **Applications:** Epidemiological studies, bacterial typing.

## 15. Biosensors:

- **Biological Components for Detection:**

  - **Antibodies, Enzymes, Nucleic Acids:** Utilized for the specific detection of microorganisms.
  - **Applications:** Environmental monitoring, food safety.

## 16. Nucleic Acid Hybridization:

- **Fluorescence in situ Hybridization (FISH):**

  - **Fluorescent Probes:** Detect specific nucleic acid sequences in microbial cells.
  - **Cellular Localization:** Allows visualization of target microorganisms.

**17. Bioluminescence Assays:**

- **Detection of Light Emission:**

  - **Luciferase Enzyme Systems:** Used for the identification and monitoring of microorganisms.
  - **Applications:** Environmental monitoring, detection of specific microbial activities.

These methods and tools collectively provide a comprehensive toolkit for microbiologists to identify, characterize, and study microorganisms in various environments and applications. The choice of method often depends on the specific goals of the study, the type of microorganism being investigated, and the available resources and expertise. Advances in technology continue to enhance the accuracy, speed, and efficiency of microbial identification techniques.

# CHAPTER SEVEN

# STRUCTURE, FUNCTION, AND CHARACTERISTICS OF MICROORGANISMS

## Introduction

Microorganisms are diverse and ubiquitous entities that play crucial roles in various ecological, industrial, and medical processes. Understanding their structure, function, and characteristics is fundamental to elucidating their roles in ecosystems, their interactions with other organisms, and their applications in biotechnology and medicine. This chapter explores the intricate world of microorganisms, encompassing bacteria, archaea, fungi, protozoa, algae, and viruses, highlighting their structural adaptations, physiological functions, and unique characteristics.

**Bacteria**

**Structural Characteristics**

Bacteria are unicellular prokaryotic microorganisms with diverse shapes, sizes, and structural features.

- **Cell Envelope**: Consists of the cell membrane, cell wall, and sometimes an outer capsule or slime layer.
- **Cell Wall**: Provides structural support and protection, composed of peptidoglycan in most bacteria.
- **Shapes**: Bacteria can be cocci (spherical), bacilli (rod-shaped), spirilla (spiral), or vibrios (comma-shaped).
- **Flagella and Pili**: External appendages involved in motility and attachment, respectively.

**Physiological Functions**

Bacteria exhibit diverse metabolic capabilities, allowing them to thrive in various environments and perform essential ecological functions.

- **Nutrient Acquisition**: Bacteria obtain energy and nutrients through diverse metabolic pathways, including aerobic respiration, anaerobic respiration, fermentation, and photosynthesis.
- **Nitrogen Fixation**: Certain bacteria, such as Rhizobium and Azotobacter, convert atmospheric nitrogen into ammonia, a form usable by plants.
- **Decomposition**: Bacteria play a crucial role in decomposing organic matter, recycling nutrients back into the ecosystem.
- **Pathogenesis**: Some bacteria are pathogens, causing diseases in plants, animals, and humans.

**Unique Characteristics**

Bacteria possess several unique characteristics that contribute to their ecological success and adaptability.

- **Endospore Formation**: Certain bacteria can form endospores, dormant structures resistant to heat, radiation, and desiccation, allowing survival in harsh conditions.
- **Horizontal Gene Transfer**: Bacteria can exchange genetic material through processes like conjugation, transformation, and transduction, contributing to genetic diversity and adaptation.
- **Quorum Sensing**: Bacteria communicate and coordinate gene expression through quorum sensing, regulating behaviors like biofilm formation and virulence.

**Archaea**

**Structural Characteristics**

Archaea are unicellular prokaryotes that differ from bacteria in their genetic, biochemical, and structural properties.

- **Cell Envelope**: Similar to bacteria, archaeal cells possess a cell membrane and sometimes a cell wall, but their cell wall composition differs from that of bacteria.
- **Unique Lipids**: Archaeal cell membranes contain unique lipid molecules, such as isoprenoid ethers, which contribute to their stability in extreme environments.
- **Shapes**: Archaea exhibit diverse shapes, including cocci, bacilli, spirilla, and irregular forms.

**Physiological Functions**

Archaea thrive in extreme environments and perform unique metabolic processes distinct from bacteria and eukaryotes.

- **Methanogenesis**: Methanogenic archaea produce methane as a metabolic byproduct, playing a crucial role in the carbon cycle.
- **Extreme Adaptations**: Archaea can survive and thrive in extreme environments, including high temperatures (thermophiles), high salinity (halophiles), and acidic or alkaline conditions.

## Unique Characteristics

Archaea possess several unique characteristics that distinguish them from bacteria and eukaryotes.

- **Genetic and Biochemical Features**: Archaeal genomes and biochemical pathways exhibit similarities to both bacteria and eukaryotes, indicating a distinct evolutionary history.
- **Extreme Environments**: Archaea are often found in extreme environments, where they contribute to nutrient cycling and primary production.
- **Biotechnological Applications**: Enzymes and metabolic pathways from extremophilic archaea have potential applications in biotechnology, such as in industrial processes and bioremediation.

## Fungi
### Structural Characteristics

Fungi are eukaryotic microorganisms with diverse morphologies and reproductive strategies.

- **Cell Wall**: Fungal cell walls contain chitin, a complex polysaccharide that provides structural support.
- **Morphological Diversity**: Fungi can be unicellular (yeasts) or multicellular (molds and mushrooms),

exhibiting various forms, including hyphae, mycelium, and fruiting bodies.

- **Reproductive Structures**: Fungi reproduce sexually and asexually through spores, which are dispersed to colonize new habitats.

## Physiological Functions

Fungi play critical roles in decomposition, nutrient cycling, symbiosis, and pathogenesis.

- **Decomposition**: Fungi decompose complex organic matter, including lignin and cellulose, releasing nutrients into the ecosystem.
- **Symbiosis**: Fungi form mutualistic relationships with plants (mycorrhizae) and algae (lichens), enhancing nutrient uptake and ecosystem resilience.
- **Pathogenesis**: Some fungi cause diseases in plants, animals, and humans, impacting ecological and economic systems.

## Unique Characteristics

Fungi exhibit several unique characteristics that contribute to their ecological and physiological roles.

- **Extracellular Digestion**: Fungi secrete enzymes into their environment to break down complex organic matter before absorbing nutrients.
- **Hyphal Growth**: Fungi grow by elongating hyphae, branching into a network called mycelium, which facilitates nutrient absorption and exploration of the environment.
- **Secondary Metabolites**: Fungi produce a wide array of secondary metabolites, including antibiotics, toxins, and

pigments, with diverse ecological and industrial applications.

**Protozoa**

**Structural Characteristics**

Protozoa are unicellular eukaryotic microorganisms with diverse morphologies and modes of locomotion.

- **Cell Structure**: Protozoa possess a nucleus and other organelles enclosed within a cell membrane.
- **Morphological Diversity**: Protozoa exhibit various shapes and structures adapted to their ecological niches, including amoeboid, ciliate, and flagellate forms.
- **Locomotion Structures**: Protozoa use structures like pseudopodia, cilia, and flagella for movement and feeding.

**Physiological Functions**

Protozoa play essential roles in nutrient cycling, predation, and symbiosis.

- **Predation**: Protozoa feed on bacteria and other microorganisms, regulating microbial populations in ecosystems.
- **Nutrient Cycling**: Through their feeding activities, protozoa contribute to nutrient cycling and the decomposition of organic matter.
- **Symbiosis**: Some protozoa form symbiotic relationships with other organisms, aiding in digestion and providing protection.

**Unique Characteristics**

Protozoa exhibit several unique characteristics that distinguish them from other microorganisms.

- **Complex Life Cycles**: Many protozoa have complex life cycles involving multiple stages, often alternating between sexual and asexual reproduction.
- **Eukaryotic Features**: Protozoa possess eukaryotic cellular structures and organelles, including a nucleus, mitochondria, and endoplasmic reticulum.
- **Adaptations to Environment**: Protozoa exhibit adaptations to diverse environments, such as mechanisms for osmoregulation and thermoregulation.

**Algae**
**Structural Characteristics**
Algae are photosynthetic eukaryotic microorganisms with diverse morphologies and pigment compositions.

- **Cell Structure**: Algae possess eukaryotic cell structures, including a nucleus, chloroplasts, and other organelles enclosed within a cell membrane.

- **Pigment Composition**: Algae contain various pigments, including chlorophyll, carotenoids, and phycobilins, which enable them to capture light energy for photosynthesis.
- **Morphological Diversity**: Algae exhibit diverse morphologies, ranging from unicellular forms (e.g., Chlamydomonas) to multicellular forms (e.g., seaweeds).
- **Cell Wall**: Algal cell walls may contain cellulose, pectin, or other polysaccharides, providing structural support and protection.

**Physiological Functions**

Algae are primary producers that play essential roles in aquatic ecosystems and global nutrient cycling.

- **Photosynthesis:** Algae perform photosynthesis, producing oxygen and organic compounds that form the base of aquatic food webs.
- **Habitat Formation**: Some algae contribute to the formation of habitats, such as coral reefs and kelp forests, providing shelter and food for diverse organisms.
- **Biogeochemical Cycling**: Algae play crucial roles in carbon, nitrogen, and phosphorus cycling, influencing nutrient availability and ecosystem productivity.

**Unique Characteristics**

Algae possess several unique characteristics that contribute to their ecological significance and diversity.

- **Unicellular and Multicellular Forms**: Algae exhibit a wide range of morphologies, from microscopic unicellular species to macroscopic multicellular forms.
- **Adaptations to Environment**: Algae have evolved adaptations to diverse environments, including strategies for buoyancy regulation, nutrient uptake, and light harvesting.
- **Secondary Metabolites**: Algae produce a variety of secondary metabolites, such as toxins and bioactive compounds, with ecological and biomedical applications.

**Viruses**
**Structural Characteristics**

Viruses are acellular entities consisting of genetic material (DNA or RNA) surrounded by a protein coat (capsid) and, in some cases, an outer lipid envelope.

- **Genetic Material**: Viruses can have either DNA or RNA as their genetic material, which may be single-stranded or double-stranded.
- **Capsid**: The protein coat (capsid) of viruses provides protection for the genetic material and determines the virus's shape and symmetry.
- **Envelope**: Some viruses have an outer lipid envelope derived from the host cell membrane, which may contain viral glycoproteins involved in host cell recognition and attachment.

**Physiological Functions**

Viruses are obligate intracellular parasites that hijack host cell machinery for replication and spread.

- **Attachment and Entry**: Viruses attach to specific receptors on host cell surfaces and enter cells through mechanisms like endocytosis or direct fusion.
- **Replication**: Once inside the host cell, viruses replicate their genetic material and synthesize viral proteins using host cell machinery.
- **Assembly and Release**: Newly synthesized viral components are assembled into complete virions, which are then released from the host cell to infect other cells.

**Unique Characteristics**

Viruses exhibit several unique characteristics that distinguish them from cellular microorganisms.

- **Obligate Intracellular Parasites**: Viruses require host cells to replicate and lack metabolic machinery of their own.
- **Genetic Diversity**: Viruses exhibit high genetic diversity due to their rapid mutation rates and potential for genetic recombination.
- **Host Specificity**: Viruses often exhibit specificity for particular host species, tissues, or cell types, dictating their tropism and pathogenicity.

Microorganisms encompass a diverse array of organisms with unique structural, functional, and ecological characteristics. Understanding the structure, function, and characteristics of microorganisms is essential for elucidating their roles in ecosystems, their interactions with other organisms, and their applications in various fields, including biotechnology, medicine, and environmental science. Continued research on microorganisms promises to yield insights into their evolutionary history, ecological significance, and potential for biotechnological innovation.

# CHAPTER EIGHT

# METHODS OF TRANSMISSION AND FACTORS INFLUENCING MICROBIAL GROWTH

## Introduction

Microorganisms, encompassing bacteria, viruses, fungi, and parasites, are ubiquitous in the environment and can have profound effects on human health. This chapter delves into the methods of transmission for different microorganisms and the myriad factors that influence their growth. By understanding these mechanisms, we can better grasp the dynamics of infectious diseases and develop effective strategies for prevention and control.

### Modes of Transmission for Different Microorganisms

1. **Direct Transmission:**

   - *Definition:* Direct transmission involves the immediate transfer of microorganisms from an infected host to a susceptible host through physical contact.
   - *Examples:* Skin-to-skin contact, sexual intercourse, and respiratory droplets.

2. **Indirect Transmission:**

   - *Definition:* Indirect transmission occurs when microorganisms are transmitted through intermediaries, such as fomites (contaminated objects or surfaces) or vectors (organisms that carry and transmit pathogens).
   - *Examples:* Contaminated surfaces, air, water, and vectors like mosquitoes.

3. **Airborne Transmission:**

   - *Definition:* Airborne transmission involves the spread of microorganisms through respiratory droplets suspended in the air.
   - *Examples:* Influenza, tuberculosis, and other respiratory infections.

4. **Foodborne Transmission:**

   - *Definition:* Foodborne transmission occurs when microorganisms are ingested through contaminated food or water.
   - *Examples:* Salmonella, E. coli, and norovirus.

5. **Vector-Borne Transmission:**

- *Definition:* Vector-borne transmission involves the use of vectors, such as mosquitoes or ticks, to transmit microorganisms from one host to another.
- *Examples:* Malaria, Lyme disease, and dengue fever.

**Environmental Factors Affecting Microbial Growth**

1. **Temperature:**

- *Impact:* Microorganisms exhibit temperature preferences for growth (psychrophiles in cold, mesophiles in moderate, and thermophiles in high temperatures).
- *Application:* Understanding temperature requirements helps control microbial growth in various environments.

2. **pH Level:**

- *Impact:* Microbial growth is influenced by the acidity or alkalinity of the environment.
- *Application:* Maintaining appropriate pH levels is crucial for controlling microbial proliferation.

3. **Moisture:**

- *Impact:* Water availability is essential for microbial growth, particularly for bacteria and fungi.
- *Application:* Proper moisture control is vital in preventing the growth of harmful microorganisms in different settings.

4. **Nutrient Availability:**

- *Impact:* Microorganisms require specific nutrients like carbon, nitrogen, and minerals for growth.
- *Application:* Understanding nutrient availability helps in managing microbial communities in various environments.

**Host Factors Influencing Susceptibility**

1. **Host Immune Response:**

- *Impact:* The immune system defends against microbial infections.
- *Application:* Immunocompromised individuals are more susceptible, emphasizing the importance of a robust immune response.

2. **Genetic Factors:**

- *Impact:* Genetic variations influence an individual's susceptibility to specific infections.
- *Application:* Identifying genetic factors aids in understanding and addressing susceptibility to diseases.

3. **Age and Sex:**

- *Impact:* Age and sex can affect immune responses, making certain groups more susceptible to infections.
- *Application:* Tailoring preventive measures for vulnerable age groups and considering sex-specific

factors in disease prevention.

## 4. Nutritional Status:

- *Impact:* Malnutrition weakens the immune system, increasing susceptibility to infections.
- *Application:* Addressing nutritional deficiencies is crucial for maintaining a robust immune response.

The methods of microbial transmission and the factors influencing microbial growth are multifaceted and interconnected. This comprehensive understanding is crucial for designing targeted interventions, implementing effective public health measures, and advancing research to combat infectious diseases. Ongoing interdisciplinary efforts will continue to refine our knowledge and enhance global resilience against microbial threats.

# CHAPTER NINE

# OVERVIEW OF THE IMMUNE SYSTEM

**Introduction**

The immune system is a marvel of biological engineering, intricately designed to protect the body from harmful pathogens while maintaining tolerance to self. In this chapter, we will do a detailed exploration of the immune system, unraveling its various components, elucidating its diverse functions, and uncovering the sophisticated regulatory mechanisms that govern its activity.

The immune system is a complex network of cells, tissues, and organs that work together to defend the body against harmful pathogens such as bacteria, viruses, fungi, and parasites. It is a critical component of our overall health, providing protection against infection and disease. In this chapter, we will delve into the intricacies of the immune system, exploring its components, functions, and the mechanisms by which it operates to safeguard the body.

**Components of the Immune System**

The immune system comprises an array of specialized cells, tissues, and organs that work synergistically to defend the body against infection and disease. Let us delve into the key components of this remarkable defense mechanism:

1. **Physical Barriers**: The first line of defense against invading pathogens includes physical barriers such as the skin, mucous membranes, and epithelial linings of the respiratory, gastrointestinal, and genitourinary tracts. These barriers serve as formidable obstacles, preventing pathogens from gaining entry into the body.

2. **Innate Immune Cells**: Phagocytes, including neutrophils, macrophages, and dendritic cells, form the backbone of the innate immune system. These cells engulf and destroy pathogens through a process called phagocytosis. Natural killer (NK) cells, another crucial component of innate immunity, target and eliminate infected or abnormal cells.

3. **Complement System**: Comprising a complex cascade of proteins, the complement system enhances the ability of antibodies and phagocytic cells to eliminate pathogens. Activation of the complement system leads to the formation of membrane attack complexes, which puncture and lyse microbial membranes.

4. **Adaptive Immune Cells**: Lymphocytes, particularly B cells and T cells, orchestrate the adaptive immune response. B cells produce antibodies that bind to specific antigens on pathogens, facilitating their neutralization and clearance. T cells, including helper T cells, cytotoxic T cells, and regulatory T cells, play diverse roles in coordinating immune responses, eliminating infected cells, and maintaining immune

homeostasis.

5. **Lymphoid Organs**: The immune system is anchored by lymphoid organs, including the bone marrow, thymus, lymph nodes, spleen, and mucosa-associated lymphoid tissues (MALT). These organs serve as hubs for the generation, maturation, and activation of immune cells, as well as sites for immune surveillance and response.

**Let us discuss the two main branches in detail: the innate immune system and the adaptive immune system.**

### 1. Innate Immune System

The innate immune system serves as the body's first line of defense against invading pathogens. It is comprised of various components, including physical barriers such as the skin and mucous membranes, as well as cellular and chemical defenses.

*Physical Barriers*: The skin and mucous membranes act as physical barriers, preventing pathogens from entering the body. The skin provides a tough, waterproof barrier, while mucous membranes secrete mucus that traps and removes pathogens.

*Cellular Defenses*: Phagocytes, such as neutrophils and macrophages, are white blood cells that engulf and destroy pathogens through a process known as phagocytosis. Natural killer (NK) cells are another type of innate immune cell that plays a role in killing infected cells and tumor cells.

*Chemical Defenses*: The innate immune system produces various chemical substances, including antimicrobial peptides and cytokines, which help to inhibit the growth and spread of pathogens.

### 2. Adaptive Immune System

The adaptive immune system, also known as acquired immunity, is highly specialized and provides targeted defense against specific pathogens. It is characterized by the presence of immune cells called lymphocytes, namely B cells and T cells, which respond to pathogens in a highly specific manner.

*Antigen Recognition*: B cells recognize pathogens through the binding of specific antigen receptors on their surface. T cells, on the other hand, recognize antigens that are presented to them by antigen-presenting cells, such as dendritic cells.

*Antibody Production*: Upon encountering a pathogen, B cells differentiate into plasma cells, which produce and secrete antibodies. Antibodies are proteins that bind to specific antigens on the surface of pathogens, marking them for destruction by other immune cells.

*Cell-Mediated Immunity*: T cells play a central role in cell-mediated immunity, which involves the direct targeting and destruction of infected or abnormal cells. There are two main types of T cells involved in cell-mediated immunity: cytotoxic T cells, which directly kill infected cells, and helper T cells, which coordinate immune responses by releasing cytokines.

**Functions of the Immune System**

The immune system performs a multitude of functions essential for safeguarding the body against microbial threats and maintaining tissue homeostasis:

1. **Recognition and Response to Pathogens**: Through the recognition of pathogen-associated molecular patterns (PAMPs) by pattern recognition receptors (PRRs), the immune system rapidly detects and responds to microbial invaders. This recognition triggers a cascade of immune responses aimed at neutralizing and eliminating pathogens.

2. **Inflammation**: Inflammation is a cornerstone of the immune response, serving as a protective mechanism to localize and eradicate pathogens, as well as to initiate tissue repair processes. The release of cytokines, chemokines, and other inflammatory mediators orchestrates the recruitment and activation of immune cells at sites of infection or injury.

3. **Immune Surveillance**: The immune system continuously surveys the body for signs of infection, malignancy, or tissue damage. Lymphocytes, particularly T cells, play a pivotal role in immune surveillance, patrolling tissues and recognizing and eliminating aberrant cells.

4. **Immune Memory**: Following exposure to pathogens or vaccination, the adaptive immune system generates immunological memory, conferring long-term protection against reinfection. Memory B cells and memory T cells retain a heightened state of readiness, enabling rapid and robust responses upon reencounter with specific antigens.

**Immune Responses**

The immune system mounts two primary types of responses to pathogens: innate immune responses and adaptive immune responses.

*Innate Immune Responses*: Innate immune responses are rapid but relatively nonspecific. They provide immediate defense against pathogens and are essential for controlling infection in the early stages. Innate immune responses include inflammation, phagocytosis, and the activation of natural killer cells.

*Adaptive Immune Responses*: Adaptive immune responses are slower to develop but are highly specific and provide long-lasting immunity against specific pathogens. These responses involve the activation of B cells and T cells, leading to the production of antibodies and the development of immunological memory.

**Immunological Memory**

One of the hallmark features of the adaptive immune system is its ability to develop immunological memory. Upon encountering a pathogen for the first time, the adaptive immune system mounts a primary immune response, which eliminates the pathogen and establishes immunity. Following this initial exposure, memory B cells and memory T cells are generated, providing long-lasting protection against reinfection with the same pathogen. This phenomenon forms the basis of vaccination, whereby exposure to a weakened or inactive form of a pathogen stimulates the immune system to produce memory cells without causing illness.

**Regulation of the Immune Response**

The immune response is finely regulated to prevent excessive inflammation, autoimmunity, or immunopathology. Several mechanisms modulate immune activity and maintain immune homeostasis:

1. **Tolerance Mechanisms**: Central tolerance mechanisms in the thymus and bone marrow ensure the deletion or functional inactivation of self-reactive lymphocytes, minimizing the risk of autoimmunity. Peripheral tolerance mechanisms, including regulatory T cells and suppressive cytokines, further dampen immune responses to self-antigens.

2. **Cytokine Regulation**: Cytokines, signaling molecules secreted by immune cells, play critical roles in modulating immune responses. Anti-inflammatory

cytokines, such as interleukin-10 (IL-10) and transforming growth factor-beta (TGF-β), counterbalance pro-inflammatory cytokines, restraining excessive inflammation and tissue damage.

3. **Checkpoints and Inhibitory Pathways**: Immune checkpoints, such as programmed cell death protein 1 (PD-1) and cytotoxic T-lymphocyte-associated protein 4 (CTLA-4), regulate T cell activation and function. Engagement of these inhibitory pathways prevents overactivation of T cells and maintains peripheral tolerance.

4. **Hormonal Regulation**: Hormones, including glucocorticoids and sex hormones, exert immunomodulatory effects, influencing immune cell development, function, and trafficking. Dysregulation of hormonal pathways can disrupt immune homeostasis and contribute to immune-related disorders.

**Dysregulation of the Immune System**

Disruption of immune homeostasis can lead to a spectrum of immune-related disorders, encompassing autoimmune diseases, immunodeficiencies, hypersensitivity reactions, and inflammatory conditions. Examples of immune disorders include rheumatoid arthritis, systemic lupus erythematosus, type 1 diabetes, allergic rhinitis, and primary immunodeficiency syndromes.

*Immunosuppression*: In certain situations, such as during pregnancy or in response to chronic infections, the immune system may undergo immunosuppression to prevent immune-mediated harm to the developing fetus or to limit tissue damage.

**Disorders of the Immune System**

Dysregulation of the immune system can lead to the development of various disorders, ranging from autoimmune diseases, where the immune system attacks the body's own tissues, to immunodeficiency disorders, where the immune system is impaired and unable to adequately protect against infections.

*Autoimmune Diseases*: Examples of autoimmune diseases include rheumatoid arthritis, systemic lupus erythematosus, and multiple sclerosis. In these conditions, the immune system mistakenly targets and attacks healthy tissues, leading to inflammation and tissue damage.

*Immunodeficiency Disorders*: Immunodeficiency disorders can be primary, resulting from genetic defects that affect the development or function of immune cells, or secondary, arising due to factors such as infections, medications, or underlying medical conditions. Examples of immunodeficiency disorders include acquired immunodeficiency syndrome (AIDS) and severe combined immunodeficiency (SCID).

The immune system plays a critical role in protecting the body against infection and disease. Comprised of a complex network of cells, tissues, and organs, the immune system employs a variety of mechanisms to detect, neutralize, and eliminate pathogens. Understanding the components and functions of the immune system is essential for developing strategies to prevent and treat immune-related disorders and to promote overall health and well-being.

# CHAPTER TEN

# DESCRIPTION OF ANTIBODIES, ANTIGENS, AND VACCINES

**1. Antigens:**

- **Types of Antigens:**

  - **Proteins:** Most antigens are proteins or glycoproteins found on the surface of pathogens.
  - **Polysaccharides:** Some antigens are composed of sugars, often found in the outer coats of bacteria.
  - **Nucleic Acids:** In some cases, DNA or RNA can act as antigens, especially in the context of certain viral infections.

- **Major Histocompatibility Complex (MHC):**

- MHC molecules present antigens to T cells, facilitating the activation of immune responses.
- MHC class I presents endogenous antigens (from within the cell), while MHC class II presents exogenous antigens (from outside the cell).

- **Self-Antigens:**

  - The immune system is designed to tolerate "self" antigens, but when tolerance breaks down, autoimmune diseases can occur.

### 2. Antibodies (Immunoglobulins):

- **Structure:**

  - Antibodies consist of four protein chains: two heavy chains and two light chains, forming a Y-shaped structure.
  - The variable regions of the antibody determine its specificity to antigens.

- **Classes of Antibodies:**

  - **IgM:** Produced in the early stages of an immune response, often as pentamers.
  - **IgG:** Predominant in secondary immune responses, provides long-term immunity.
  - **IgA:** Found in mucosal secretions, protecting mucous membranes.
  - **IgE:** Involved in allergic responses and defense against parasites.

- **Antibody Functions:**

  - **Agglutination:** Antibodies can clump pathogens together, making them easier targets for phagocytes.
  - **Precipitation:** Antibodies can cause soluble antigens to aggregate and precipitate, facilitating their removal.
  - **Activation of Complement:** Antibodies can trigger the complement system, leading to the lysis of pathogens.

### 3. Vaccines:

- **Types of Vaccines:**

  - **Inactivated Vaccines:** Pathogens are killed or inactivated, often by heat or chemicals.
  - **Live Attenuated Vaccines:** Weakened forms of live pathogens that do not cause disease in healthy individuals.
  - **Subunit, Recombinant, or Conjugate Vaccines:** Contain specific parts of the pathogen, such as proteins or sugars.

- **Adjuvants:**

  - Substances added to vaccines to enhance the immune response.
  - They stimulate a more robust and long-lasting reaction.

- **Memory Cells:**

- Memory B cells "remember" the antigens encountered during vaccination.
- Memory T cells are also crucial for a rapid immune response upon re-exposure.

- **Herd Immunity:**

  - Occurs when a significant portion of the population is immune, reducing the spread of the disease.
  - Protects those who are unable to receive vaccines, such as individuals with certain medical conditions.

**4. Interactions and Specificity:**

- **Antigen-Antibody Interaction:**

  - Antibodies recognize and bind to antigens with high specificity through the variable regions.
  - This specificity ensures that each antibody is tailored to a particular antigen.

- **Clonal Selection:**

  - The immune system selectively activates B cells that produce antibodies specific to the encountered antigen.
  - This process leads to the production of a large population of identical B cells, ensuring a focused immune response.

**Role of antibodies, antigens, and vaccines**
**Roles of Antigens:**

1. **Identification of Pathogens:**

   - Antigens act as molecular markers on the surface of pathogens, allowing the immune system to distinguish between self and non-self.
   - The immune system recognizes these foreign antigens as signals to mount a defense against potential threats.

2. **Immune System Activation:**

   - Antigens trigger the activation of immune responses, leading to the production of antibodies and the deployment of other immune cells.
   - The immune system's recognition of antigens is a crucial step in initiating an effective defense against infections.

3. **Memory Formation:**

   - Antigen exposure results in the formation of memory cells (memory B cells and memory T cells), providing long-lasting immunity.
   - Memory cells "remember" specific antigens, allowing the immune system to respond rapidly upon re-exposure to the same pathogen.

**Roles of Antibodies (Immunoglobulins):**

1. **Neutralization of Pathogens:**

   - Antibodies bind to pathogens, preventing them from entering or infecting host cells.

- This neutralization reduces the ability of pathogens to cause harm and aids in their subsequent elimination.

2. **Opsonization and Phagocytosis:**

- Antibodies tag pathogens for recognition by phagocytic cells such as macrophages and neutrophils.
- This process, known as opsonization, enhances the efficiency of phagocytosis, leading to the removal of the marked pathogens.

3. **Activation of Complement System:**

- Antibodies can activate the complement system, a cascade of proteins that amplify the immune response.
- Complement activation leads to the lysis of pathogens, inflammation, and enhanced clearance by immune cells.

4. **Agglutination and Precipitation:**

- Antibodies can cause pathogens to clump together (agglutination) or precipitate, facilitating their removal from the body.
- These processes aid in the elimination of pathogens by making them more accessible to immune cells.

5. **Crossing the Placenta:**

- Certain antibody classes, such as IgG, can cross the placenta from a pregnant woman to her fetus, providing passive immunity to the newborn.

**Roles of Vaccines:**

1. **Stimulation of Immune Response:**

   - Vaccines contain antigens (either inactivated or weakened forms) that mimic pathogens without causing the disease.
   - Upon vaccination, the immune system recognizes these antigens and mounts an immune response, including the production of antibodies.

2. **Memory Cell Formation:**

   - Vaccination leads to the development of memory B cells and memory T cells, ensuring a faster and more robust immune response upon subsequent exposure to the actual pathogen.

3. **Prevention of Disease Spread:**

   - Mass vaccination programs contribute to the establishment of herd immunity, reducing the spread of infectious diseases within communities.
   - Herd immunity protects vulnerable individuals who may be unable to receive vaccines.

4. **Long-Term Protection:**

- Vaccination provides long-lasting protection against specific diseases, reducing the severity of illness and the risk of complications.

## 5. Global Public Health Impact:

- Vaccines have played a crucial role in controlling and eradicating infectious diseases globally, significantly improving public health outcomes.

# CHAPTER ELEVEN

# IMMUNE RESPONSE TO VARIOUS COMMUNICABLE DISEASES

**Introduction**

Communicable diseases, also known as infectious diseases, are illnesses caused by microorganisms such as bacteria, viruses, fungi, or parasites. These diseases can spread from person to person through various means, including direct contact, airborne transmission, or ingestion of contaminated food or water. The human immune system plays a vital role in defending against these pathogens, employing a complex array of mechanisms to identify, neutralize, and eliminate invaders. This chapter aims to delve into the immune responses mounted against various communicable diseases, highlighting the intricacies of host-pathogen interactions and the role of immunity in combating infections.

## 1. Innate Immune Response

The innate immune system serves as the body's first line of defense against pathogens. It comprises physical barriers such as the skin and mucous membranes, as well as cellular and molecular components that recognize and respond to foreign invaders promptly.

a. Recognition of Pathogens: Pattern Recognition Receptors (PRRs) expressed on immune cells detect conserved molecular patterns present in pathogens, triggering an immediate response.

b. Inflammatory Response: Upon detection of pathogens, immune cells release cytokines and chemokines, initiating inflammation to contain and eliminate the infection.

c. Phagocytosis: Phagocytes, including neutrophils, macrophages, and dendritic cells, engulf and digest pathogens through phagocytosis, clearing the infection.

## 1. Adaptive Immune Response

The adaptive immune system provides a targeted and specific response to pathogens, characterized by the recognition of unique antigens and the generation of immunological memory for future protection.

a. Antigen Presentation:

Antigen-presenting cells (APCs), such as dendritic cells and macrophages, process and present pathogen-derived antigens to T lymphocytes, initiating adaptive immune responses.

b.  T Cell-Mediated Immunity:

Helper T cells (Th) orchestrate immune responses by releasing cytokines and activating other immune cells. Cytotoxic T cells (Tc) directly kill infected cells, while regulatory T cells (Treg) modulate immune responses to prevent excessive inflammation.

c.  B Cell-Mediated Immunity:

B lymphocytes produce antibodies (immunoglobulins) specific to pathogen antigens, facilitating pathogen neutralization, opsonization, and activation of the complement system.

3. **Immune Response to Specific Communicable Diseases**

a. Viral Infections:
i. Influenza:
The immune response targets viral proteins, including hemagglutinin and neuraminidase, to neutralize the virus and clear infected cells.
ii. HIV/AIDS:
HIV evades immune detection and attacks CD4+ T cells, leading to immunodeficiency. Antiretroviral therapy helps control viral replication and preserve immune function.
iii. COVID-19:
SARS-CoV-2 infection elicits a multifaceted immune response involving both innate and adaptive components. Severe cases are characterized by dysregulated

inflammation and cytokine storm.

b. Bacterial Infections:

i. Tuberculosis:

Mycobacterium tuberculosis evades immune surveillance by residing within macrophages. Granuloma formation helps contain the infection, but chronic inflammation can lead to tissue damage.

ii. Streptococcal Infections:

Group A Streptococcus (GAS) triggers a robust inflammatory response, contributing to tissue damage and systemic complications such as rheumatic fever and post-streptococcal glomerulonephritis.

c. Parasitic Infections:

i. Malaria:

Plasmodium parasites evade immune detection through antigenic variation and sequestration within host cells. Adaptive immune responses targeting specific parasite antigens confer partial immunity upon repeated exposure.

ii. Leishmaniasis:

Leishmania parasites evade immune clearance by residing within host macrophages. Th1-mediated responses are crucial for controlling infection, while Th2 responses exacerbate disease progression.

## 4. Immunization and Immune Memory

Immunization strategies, including vaccination, aim to stimulate protective immune responses against specific pathogens, thereby preventing infection and reducing disease burden. Vaccines induce immunological memory, enabling rapid and robust responses upon subsequent exposure to the pathogen. Vaccination campaigns have played a pivotal role in controlling communicable diseases worldwide, leading to the eradication or near-elimination of diseases such as smallpox and polio.

The immune response to communicable diseases is a dynamic interplay between host defenses and microbial pathogens. Understanding the intricacies of immune responses against various infectious agents is essential for developing effective preventive and therapeutic interventions. Continued research into host-pathogen interactions and immune modulation will pave the way for innovative strategies to combat communicable diseases and safeguard public health.

# CHAPTER TWELVE

# IMPORTANCE OF HERD IMMUNITY

**Introduction**

Herd immunity, also known as community immunity, is a critical concept in public health that describes the indirect protection from infectious diseases conferred to a population when a sufficiently high proportion of individuals are immune. This immunity can result from previous infection or vaccination, effectively reducing the spread of pathogens within a community. Understanding the importance of herd immunity is paramount in designing and implementing effective disease control strategies. This chapter explores the principles, implications, and challenges associated with achieving and maintaining herd immunity.

1. **Principles of Herd Immunity**

   a. **Threshold for Protection:**

The level of immunity required to achieve herd immunity varies depending on the contagiousness of the infectious agent, often quantified by the basic reproduction number (R0). For highly contagious diseases like measles, a high vaccination coverage approaching 95% is necessary to interrupt transmission.

### a.  Breaking Transmission Chains:

Herd immunity disrupts the transmission of pathogens within a population by reducing the likelihood of susceptible individuals encountering infectious individuals. This not only protects vulnerable individuals who cannot be vaccinated but also helps control outbreaks and prevent epidemics.

### c.  Protection of Vulnerable Populations:

Individuals who cannot receive vaccines due to medical reasons, such as infants, elderly individuals, or those with compromised immune systems, rely on herd immunity for protection against vaccine-preventable diseases.

## 2.  Achieving Herd Immunity Through Vaccination

### a.  Vaccine Coverage:

Vaccination programs aim to achieve high population coverage to establish and maintain herd immunity. Routine immunization schedules target specific age groups, while catch-up campaigns and mass vaccination efforts address gaps in coverage.

### b.  Vaccine Efficacy and Effectiveness:

The effectiveness of vaccination in conferring immunity varies depending on factors such as vaccine formulation, schedule, and population characteristics. Monitoring vaccine coverage and evaluating vaccine efficacy are essential for assessing the impact of immunization programs on herd immunity.

c.  **Vaccine Hesitancy and Barriers:**

Vaccine hesitancy, fueled by misinformation, mistrust, and complacency, poses a significant challenge to achieving herd immunity. Addressing vaccine-related misconceptions, enhancing access to vaccines, and fostering trust in immunization are crucial for overcoming barriers to vaccination uptake.

3.  **Natural Immunity and Herd Protection**

a.  **Disease Outbreaks and Epidemics:**

In the absence of vaccination, natural immunity acquired through previous infection can contribute to herd immunity. However, relying solely on natural infection for immunity comes at the cost of increased morbidity, mortality, and societal disruption due to disease outbreaks and epidemics.

b.  **Challenges of Natural Immunity:**

Reliance on natural immunity for herd protection is associated with significant health risks, particularly for diseases with severe consequences or long-term complications. Furthermore, achieving herd immunity through natural infection entails a high burden of illness and places strain on healthcare systems.

## 4. Challenges and Considerations

### a. Global Disparities in Immunization:

Disparities in vaccine access, coverage, and healthcare infrastructure pose challenges to achieving and maintaining herd immunity, particularly in resource-limited settings. International cooperation and investment in global immunization efforts are essential for addressing these disparities.

### b. Emerging Infectious Threats:

The emergence of novel pathogens, antimicrobial resistance, and vaccine-evading variants underscore the importance of proactive surveillance, research, and preparedness to safeguard herd immunity against evolving infectious threats.

### c. Sustaining Vaccine Confidence:

Building and maintaining public trust in vaccines and immunization programs requires ongoing communication, transparency, and collaboration between healthcare providers, policymakers, and communities.

Herd immunity is a cornerstone of public health, offering protection against infectious diseases at the population level. Achieving and maintaining herd immunity requires concerted efforts to promote vaccination uptake, address vaccine hesitancy, and strengthen healthcare systems. By prioritizing immunization as a collective responsibility, communities can effectively safeguard public health and mitigate the impact of infectious diseases.

# CHAPTER THIRTEEN

# BASICS OF EPIDEMIOLOGY AND DISEASE SURVEILLANCE

**Introduction**

Epidemiology, the study of the distribution and determinants of diseases in populations, serves as a cornerstone of public health practice. Disease surveillance, a vital component of epidemiology, involves systematic collection, analysis, and interpretation of health-related data to inform public health action. This chapter elucidates the basics of epidemiology and disease surveillance, exploring key concepts, methods, and applications in disease control and prevention.

1. **Key Concepts in Epidemiology**

   a. Disease Occurrence:

Epidemiologists quantify the occurrence of diseases using measures such as incidence (new cases over a defined period) and prevalence (total cases in a population at a specific time). Understanding disease burden helps prioritize interventions and allocate resources effectively.

a.  Determinants of Health:

Epidemiology investigates factors influencing disease occurrence, including biological, environmental, behavioral, and social determinants. Identifying modifiable risk factors informs preventive strategies and health promotion initiatives.

c.  Study Designs:

Epidemiological studies employ various designs, including observational (e.g., cohort, case-control) and experimental (e.g., clinical trials), to investigate associations between exposures and outcomes. Each study design has strengths and limitations in establishing causality and generalizability.

2.  **Principles of Disease Surveillance**

a.  Surveillance Objectives:

Disease surveillance aims to monitor disease trends, detect outbreaks, assess the impact of interventions, and guide public health policies. Timeliness, completeness, and representativeness of surveillance data are essential for effective decision-making.

b.  Surveillance Systems:

Surveillance systems collect data from multiple sources, including healthcare facilities, laboratories, and population surveys. Integration of data from diverse sources enhances the sensitivity and specificity of surveillance for detecting health threats.

c.  Syndromic Surveillance:

Syndromic surveillance monitors patterns of symptoms or clinical presentations in real-time to detect outbreaks or unusual health events promptly. Rapid detection facilitates early response and containment of infectious diseases and other public health emergencies.

3.  **Disease Outbreak Investigation**

a.  Outbreak Detection:

Epidemiologists investigate clusters of cases or unusual patterns of disease through surveillance data analysis and field investigations. Epidemiological tools such as case definitions, contact tracing, and environmental assessments aid in outbreak detection and characterization.

b.  Case-Control Studies:

Case-control studies compare exposures between cases (individuals with the disease) and controls (individuals without the disease) to identify potential risk factors associated with the outbreak. Analyzing exposures and outcomes helps elucidate the source and transmission of the disease.

c.  Intervention Strategies:

Outbreak response strategies may include implementing control measures (e.g., quarantine, isolation), enhancing surveillance and case finding, and communicating risk to the public. Multidisciplinary collaboration among public health agencies, healthcare providers, and communities is essential for effective outbreak control.

4. **Applications of Epidemiology and Disease Surveillance**

a.  Disease Prevention:

Epidemiological findings inform preventive measures such as vaccination, vector control, and health education programs. Targeted interventions based on epidemiological evidence reduce disease incidence and improve population health outcomes.

b.  Policy Development:

Epidemiological data guides policy development at local, national, and global levels, shaping public health priorities, resource allocation, and regulatory decisions. Evidence-based policymaking promotes effective disease control and public health promotion initiatives.

c.  Global Health Security:

Epidemiology and disease surveillance play a crucial role in global health security by detecting emerging infectious threats, monitoring antimicrobial resistance, and facilitating coordinated responses to pandemics and other health emergencies.

Epidemiology and disease surveillance are indispensable tools for understanding disease patterns, identifying risk factors, and guiding public health interventions. By applying epidemiological principles and surveillance methodologies, public health practitioners can effectively monitor, control, and prevent diseases, thereby improving the health and well-being of populations worldwide.

# CHAPTER FOURTEEN

# OUTBREAK INVESTIGATION AND CONTACT TRACING

**Introduction**

Outbreak investigation and contact tracing are fundamental public health strategies employed to detect, contain, and mitigate the spread of infectious diseases. These processes involve a systematic approach to identify cases, track transmission chains, and implement control measures. This chapter delves into the intricacies of outbreak investigation and contact tracing, highlighting their importance in disease control and public health response.

1.  **Outbreak Investigation**

    a.  Detection and Notification:

Outbreaks may be detected through routine surveillance systems, unusual patterns of disease, or reports from healthcare providers or the public. Timely notification and communication are critical for initiating an effective response.

a.  Case Definition:

Defining cases based on clinical, epidemiological, and laboratory criteria helps standardize case identification and facilitate data collection. Case definitions evolve as new information becomes available during the investigation.

c.  Case Identification and Confirmation:

Epidemiologists identify and confirm cases through clinical assessment, laboratory testing, and epidemiological linkage. Rapid diagnosis and confirmation enable prompt intervention and control measures.

2.  **Steps in Outbreak Investigation**

a.  Establishing the Existence of an Outbreak:

Epidemiologists assess the magnitude, severity, and geographic distribution of cases to determine if an outbreak is occurring. Statistical methods, such as epidemic curves and spatial analysis, aid in identifying clusters of cases.

b.  Formulating Hypotheses:

Epidemiological investigations generate hypotheses about the source, mode of transmission, and risk factors associated with the outbreak. Hypotheses guide data collection, analysis, and hypothesis testing to elucidate the outbreak's cause.

c. Conducting Epidemiological Studies:

Case-control studies, cohort studies, and other analytical methods are employed to investigate associations between exposures and outcomes. Epidemiologists examine demographic, clinical, and behavioral characteristics of cases and controls to identify potential risk factors.

3. **Contact Tracing**

a. Definition of Contacts:

Contacts are individuals who have been exposed to an infectious case during the period of communicability. Contact tracing aims to identify, notify, and monitor contacts to prevent secondary transmission and interrupt disease spread.

b. Tracing Process:

Contact tracing involves interviewing cases to identify contacts, obtaining contact information, and notifying contacts of their exposure. Contacts may undergo risk assessment, testing, and quarantine or isolation measures based on their level of exposure and the infectious agent's characteristics.

c. Digital Contact Tracing:

Digital technologies, including mobile applications and electronic databases, streamline contact tracing processes by automating case and contact identification, notification, and monitoring. Privacy considerations and data security are paramount in digital contact tracing initiatives.

## 4. Challenges and Considerations

a. Resource Constraints:

Outbreak investigations and contact tracing efforts require adequate staffing, expertise, laboratory support, and logistical resources. Resource constraints can impede timely response and hinder effective control measures.

b. Community Engagement:

Building trust, addressing misconceptions, and engaging communities are essential for successful outbreak investigations and contact tracing. Culturally sensitive communication and community involvement enhance cooperation and compliance with public health recommendations.

c. Ethical Considerations:

Ethical principles, including confidentiality, informed consent, and respect for autonomy, guide outbreak response activities and contact tracing efforts. Balancing individual rights with public health imperatives is crucial in implementing ethical and equitable interventions.

Outbreak investigation and contact tracing are integral components of infectious disease control, enabling rapid detection, containment, and mitigation of outbreaks. By employing systematic approaches, leveraging epidemiological methods, and fostering collaboration across sectors, public health authorities can effectively respond to outbreaks and safeguard population health. Continuous refinement of outbreak response strategies and investments in surveillance infrastructure strengthen preparedness and resilience against emerging infectious threats.

# CHAPTER FIFTEEN

# Strategies for Communicable Disease Prevention and Control

**Introduction**

Preventing and controlling communicable diseases is a multifaceted endeavor that requires coordinated efforts across various sectors of society. Effective strategies encompass a range of interventions, including vaccination, vector control, health promotion, and surveillance. This chapter explores key strategies for preventing and controlling communicable diseases, emphasizing the importance of integrated approaches in reducing disease burden and promoting public health.

1.  **Vaccination and Immunization**

a. *Importance of Vaccination:*

Vaccination is one of the most cost-effective public health interventions for preventing infectious diseases. Vaccines stimulate the immune system to produce protective immunity against specific pathogens, thereby reducing the risk of infection and transmission within communities.

a. *Vaccination Programs:*

National immunization programs administer vaccines to target populations based on age, risk factors, and disease burden. Routine immunization schedules, catch-up campaigns, and mass vaccination initiatives aim to achieve high vaccination coverage and establish herd immunity.

c. *Vaccine Development and Deployment:*

Research and development efforts focus on developing new vaccines, improving vaccine efficacy and safety, and expanding vaccine coverage to underserved populations. Effective vaccine distribution networks ensure equitable access to vaccines and reach remote or marginalized communities.

## 2. Vector Control and Environmental Management

a. *Vector-Borne Diseases:*

Vector control measures target arthropods such as mosquitoes, ticks, and flies that transmit pathogens causing diseases like malaria, dengue fever, and Zika virus infection. Strategies include insecticide spraying, larval source reduction, and use of bed nets and repellents to prevent bites.

b. ***Integrated Vector Management (IVM):***

IVM combines multiple vector control interventions with environmental management and community engagement to achieve sustainable reductions in vector populations and disease transmission. IVM strategies are tailored to local ecological, epidemiological, and socio-economic contexts.

c. ***Climate Change Adaptation:***

Climate change influences vector distribution, abundance, and disease transmission dynamics, posing challenges to vector control efforts. Adaptation strategies, such as early warning systems, habitat modification, and community resilience-building, mitigate the impact of climate-related changes on vector-borne diseases.

3. **Health Promotion and Behavior Change**

a. ***Risk Communication:***

Effective risk communication strategies disseminate accurate, timely, and understandable information to the public about disease risks, preventive measures, and recommended behaviors. Clear messaging builds trust, fosters cooperation, and empowers individuals to take proactive steps to protect their health.

### b. *Health Education:*

Health education programs raise awareness about communicable diseases, modes of transmission, and preventive measures through targeted interventions in schools, communities, and healthcare settings. Education campaigns promote behaviors such as hand hygiene, vaccination, and safe sexual practices.

### c. *Social and Behavioral Interventions:*

Social and behavioral interventions address underlying determinants of health, including poverty, gender inequality, and social exclusion, which influence disease vulnerability and transmission. Empowering communities, promoting equitable access to healthcare, and addressing stigma and discrimination enhance resilience to communicable diseases.

## 4. Surveillance and Early Warning Systems

### a. *Disease Surveillance:*

Surveillance systems monitor disease trends, detect outbreaks, and assess the effectiveness of control measures through systematic collection, analysis, and interpretation of health data. Integrated surveillance networks combine clinical, laboratory, and epidemiological data to provide comprehensive situational awareness.

### b. *Early Warning Systems:*

Early warning systems use epidemiological, environmental, and social indicators to forecast disease outbreaks and public health emergencies. Predictive modeling, syndromic surveillance, and real-time data analysis enable timely response and allocation of resources to high-risk areas.

### c. *Global Health Security:*

Strengthening global health security involves enhancing surveillance capacities, building laboratory infrastructure, and fostering collaboration among countries to detect, prevent, and respond to communicable diseases with pandemic potential. International frameworks, such as the International Health Regulations (IHR), facilitate coordination and information sharing to mitigate cross-border health threats.

Preventing and controlling communicable diseases requires a comprehensive approach that addresses biological, environmental, social, and behavioral determinants of health. By implementing evidence-based interventions, strengthening health systems, and fostering multisectoral collaboration, communities can reduce the burden of infectious diseases and promote health equity for all. Continued investment in disease prevention and control efforts is essential for achieving sustainable improvements in global health outcomes.

# CHAPTER SIXTEEN

# CASE STUDIES ON SUCCESSFUL DISEASE ERADICATION PROGRAMS

**Introduction**

Disease eradication represents one of the most formidable and rewarding challenges in public health. The complete and permanent worldwide reduction to zero new cases of an infectious disease signifies not only a triumph of medical science but also a testament to human perseverance, international cooperation, and robust health systems. This chapter explores notable examples of successful disease eradication, distills lessons learned from these campaigns, and discusses ongoing challenges in global disease control.

**Notable Examples of Disease Eradication**
**Smallpox**

## Background

Smallpox, caused by the Variola virus, was one of the deadliest diseases known to humanity. It caused severe fever and a distinctive skin rash that left survivors with significant scarring and, often, blindness. Historical records indicate that smallpox has afflicted humanity for at least 3,000 years, causing hundreds of millions of deaths in the 20th century alone.

## Eradication Campaign

The global campaign to eradicate smallpox began in earnest in 1959, led by the World Health Organization (WHO). Early efforts focused on mass vaccination, but logistical challenges and limited resources slowed progress. A breakthrough came with the development of the bifurcated needle in the 1960s, which allowed for more efficient and effective vaccination. The strategy shifted to "surveillance and containment," where health workers quickly identified and isolated cases, vaccinating those in close contact to prevent spread.

By the late 1970s, these efforts culminated in the eradication of smallpox. The last naturally occurring case was recorded in Somalia in 1977, and in 1980, WHO declared smallpox eradicated, marking a historic achievement.

## Key Strategies

- **Mass Vaccination:** The introduction of the bifurcated needle was a game-changer, enabling more people to be vaccinated quickly and efficiently.
- **Surveillance and Containment:** Rapid identification, isolation, and vaccination of contacts prevented outbreaks from spreading.

- **Global Coordination:** International cooperation and funding were crucial, with countries working together to share information and resources.

## Rinderpest

### Background

Rinderpest, also known as cattle plague, was a viral disease that devastated livestock populations, particularly cattle, causing high mortality rates. It had severe economic impacts, especially in regions where agriculture and livestock were critical to livelihoods.

### Eradication Campaign

The Global Rinderpest Eradication Programme (GREP) was launched by the Food and Agriculture Organization (FAO) of the United Nations in 1994. This program built on earlier efforts that had significantly reduced the prevalence of the disease. Key strategies included widespread vaccination campaigns, establishment of strong surveillance systems, and training for veterinarians and farmers to recognize and respond to outbreaks. The program's success led to the declaration of rinderpest eradication in 2011.

### Key Strategies

- **Vaccination Campaigns:** Development and distribution of effective vaccines were central to controlling and eventually eradicating the disease.
- **Surveillance Networks:** Establishing robust surveillance systems allowed for quick detection and response to outbreaks, preventing spread.
- **Education and Training:** Training veterinarians and farmers in disease recognition and response ensured rapid action at the local level.

## Lessons Learned from Successful Campaigns

### Political and Community Engagement

Effective disease eradication requires not only medical and scientific efforts but also strong political commitment and community engagement. Governments must prioritize eradication programs, providing the necessary political backing and resources. Community leaders and members must be educated about the disease and involved in the eradication efforts to ensure compliance and cooperation. For instance, the success of smallpox eradication was partly due to the engagement of local communities in surveillance and vaccination efforts, ensuring high levels of participation and support.

### Robust Surveillance Systems

Accurate and timely data are critical for tracking disease outbreaks and assessing the effectiveness of eradication efforts. Strong surveillance systems enable rapid detection and response to new cases, preventing the spread of the disease. The "surveillance and containment" strategy used in smallpox eradication is a prime example, where continuous monitoring and immediate action were essential to prevent outbreaks from spreading.

### Adequate Funding and Resources

Sustainable funding is essential for the continuity and success of eradication programs. Financial constraints can lead to interruptions in vaccination campaigns and surveillance activities, jeopardizing progress. The eradication of smallpox was supported by significant international funding, ensuring that resources were available to maintain the intensity and reach of the campaign until the disease was eliminated.

### Global Collaboration

Diseases do not recognize borders; thus, international collaboration is paramount. Sharing information, resources, and best practices among countries enhances the effectiveness of eradication efforts. Global health organizations play a crucial role in coordinating these efforts. The eradication of rinderpest, for example, was achieved through the collaborative efforts of multiple countries, facilitated by the FAO, which coordinated activities and ensured consistent implementation of strategies worldwide.

**Adaptability and Innovation**

Flexibility and innovation are crucial for overcoming challenges that arise during eradication campaigns. Developing new technologies, such as more effective vaccines and diagnostic tools, and adapting strategies based on local contexts contribute to the success of eradication programs. The development of the bifurcated needle for smallpox vaccination and the innovative surveillance methods for rinderpest are examples of how adaptability and technological advances can drive success.

**Ongoing Challenges in Global Disease Control**

**Emerging and Re-emerging Diseases**

New pathogens continue to emerge, and previously controlled diseases can resurface. Factors such as global travel, urbanization, climate change, and antimicrobial resistance contribute to the complexity of disease control. Continuous vigilance, research, and adaptation of strategies are necessary to address these threats. For example, diseases like Ebola and Zika have emerged as significant public health threats in recent years, requiring swift international response and innovative approaches to containment and control.

**Vaccine Hesitancy**

Vaccine hesitancy, fueled by misinformation and distrust in health authorities, poses a significant challenge to disease control efforts. Public health campaigns must address these concerns through transparent communication, community engagement, and education to build trust and promote vaccination. The resurgence of diseases like measles in some parts of the world highlights the impact of vaccine hesitancy on public health.

## Weak Health Systems

In many parts of the world, health systems are under-resourced and lack the infrastructure necessary for effective disease control. Strengthening health systems, including improving access to healthcare, training healthcare workers, and enhancing laboratory capacity, is essential for the success of eradication and control programs. In regions with weak health systems, outbreaks of diseases like cholera and tuberculosis continue to pose significant challenges.

## Conflict and Political Instability

Conflict and political instability can disrupt health services, making it difficult to implement and sustain disease control measures. Efforts must be made to provide healthcare in conflict zones and to negotiate ceasefires or health-related truces to allow vaccination and treatment efforts to proceed. For instance, polio eradication efforts in countries like Afghanistan and Pakistan have faced significant hurdles due to ongoing conflict and insecurity.

## Equity and Access

Ensuring equitable access to healthcare services and interventions is critical for disease eradication. Marginalized and vulnerable populations often face barriers to accessing care, which can hinder eradication efforts. Addressing social determinants of health and ensuring inclusive and equitable health policies are vital for the success of disease control programs. The disparity in access to healthcare and vaccines between high-income and low-income countries underscores the need for global efforts to ensure health equity.

The eradication of diseases like smallpox and rinderpest stands as a testament to what can be achieved through concerted global efforts. These successes provide valuable lessons for current and future eradication and disease control initiatives. However, significant challenges remain, and continued investment in research, surveillance, and health systems is essential to address emerging threats and achieve global health goals. The journey towards eradicating diseases is arduous and complex, but with sustained commitment, innovation, and collaboration, it is a journey that holds the promise of a healthier future for all.

# CHAPTER SEVENTEEN

# ROLE OF PUBLIC HEALTH IN PREVENTING AND MANAGING COMMUNICABLE DISEASES

**Introduction**

Public health plays a crucial role in preventing and managing communicable diseases, which continue to pose significant threats to global health. Through robust public health infrastructure, interdisciplinary approaches, and effective public awareness and education programs, public health systems work to mitigate the spread of infectious diseases and safeguard communities. This chapter explores the key components and strategies involved in the public health response to communicable diseases.

## Public Health Infrastructure and Its Role

### *Surveillance Systems*

*Case Reporting*

Case reporting is a fundamental component of surveillance systems. Healthcare providers, including doctors, nurses, and public health officials, are required to report cases of certain communicable diseases to public health authorities. This process ensures that cases are detected early and responded to promptly. Effective case reporting relies on clear guidelines and standardized forms to capture essential data.

*Early Detection*

Prompt reporting helps identify outbreaks at an early stage, allowing for immediate intervention.

*Data Standardization*

Consistent data collection methods ensure comparability and reliability of information across different regions and time periods.

### *Laboratory Networks*

Laboratories play a critical role in diagnosing diseases, confirming outbreaks, and identifying causative agents. Collaborative networks of laboratories enhance diagnostic capacity and ensure accurate and timely results.

*Diagnostic Accuracy*

Advanced laboratory techniques enable precise identification of pathogens, which is essential for appropriate treatment and control measures.

*Collaboration and Information Sharing*

Networks of laboratories facilitate the exchange of information and resources, strengthening overall diagnostic capabilities.

### *Digital Health Technologies*

Advances in technology have significantly improved surveillance capabilities. Digital tools, such as electronic health records (EHRs) and mobile applications, facilitate real-time data collection and analysis.

*Electronic Health Records (EHRs)*

EHRs streamline the collection and sharing of patient information, improving the accuracy and efficiency of surveillance.

*Mobile Applications*

Mobile apps enable health workers and the public to report symptoms and receive updates, enhancing community-level surveillance.

## Immunization Programs

### Routine Immunization

Routine immunization programs are designed to protect individuals, particularly children, against a range of infectious diseases. These programs follow a scheduled series of vaccinations to ensure immunity is built up over time.

*Childhood Vaccination*

Programs targeting diseases such as measles, mumps, rubella, diphtheria, and pertussis are critical in reducing childhood morbidity and mortality.

*Adult Immunization*

Vaccination schedules for adults, including seasonal flu vaccines and boosters for tetanus and diphtheria, help maintain immunity throughout life.

### Mass Vaccination Campaigns

During outbreaks or efforts to eliminate specific diseases, mass vaccination campaigns are launched to achieve high coverage quickly. These campaigns often target specific populations or regions at high risk.

### Emergency Response

Mass campaigns are crucial during public health emergencies, such as outbreaks of polio or cholera.

### Community Mobilization

Engaging communities in mass vaccination efforts ensures higher participation and success rates.

### Herd Immunity

Achieving high vaccination coverage within a community provides indirect protection to unvaccinated individuals, reducing the overall spread of disease. Herd immunity is essential for protecting vulnerable populations, such as those who cannot be vaccinated due to medical conditions.

*Threshold Coverage:*

The level of vaccination needed to achieve herd immunity varies by disease, typically ranging from 70% to 95%.

*Protecting the Vulnerable:*

High community immunity levels help protect those who are immune-compromised, infants, and the elderly.

### Public Health Workforce

### Epidemiologists

Epidemiologists are essential for investigating outbreaks, identifying sources of infection, and recommending control measures. Their work involves data analysis, field investigations, and developing public health policies.

**Outbreak Investigation:** Epidemiologists track the spread of disease, identify affected populations, and determine the source of outbreaks.

**Data Analysis:** They analyze surveillance data to identify trends, risk factors, and the effectiveness of interventions.

### Health Educators

Health educators develop and disseminate educational materials to inform the public about disease prevention and healthy behaviors. Their work is crucial in promoting health literacy and encouraging preventive practices.

**Educational Campaigns:** Health educators design campaigns to raise awareness about vaccination, hygiene, and disease prevention.

**Community Engagement:** They work with community leaders and organizations to tailor messages and ensure they reach diverse audiences effectively.

### Environmental Health Specialists

Environmental health specialists address environmental factors that contribute to disease transmission, such as water quality, sanitation, and food safety. Their work involves inspections, regulations, and public education.

**Water and Sanitation:** Ensuring access to clean water and proper sanitation facilities reduces the risk of waterborne diseases.

**Food Safety:** Implementing food safety standards and conducting inspections prevent the spread of foodborne illnesses.

### Health Infrastructure

*Healthcare Facilities*

Hospitals, clinics, and other healthcare facilities provide treatment and care for individuals with infectious diseases. They also play a vital role in reporting cases and administering vaccines.

*Inpatient and Outpatient Care*

Facilities offer both emergency care for severe cases and routine outpatient services for disease management.

*Infection Control*

Implementing strict infection control protocols in healthcare settings prevents nosocomial (hospital-acquired) infections.

### *Diagnostic Laboratories*

Diagnostic laboratories are crucial for identifying pathogens, conducting tests, and supporting epidemiological investigations. They ensure accurate diagnosis and monitoring of disease trends.

*Advanced Diagnostics*

Utilizing molecular techniques, such as PCR and genome sequencing, enhances the accuracy and speed of pathogen identification.

*Surveillance Support*

Laboratories contribute to ongoing surveillance efforts by providing data on pathogen prevalence and resistance patterns.

### *Public Health Institutions*

Organizations like the Centers for Disease Control and Prevention (CDC) and the World Health Organization (WHO) coordinate efforts, provide guidelines, and support countries in managing public health threats.

*Global Coordination*

Public health institutions facilitate international collaboration and resource sharing during outbreaks.

*Guidelines and Protocols*

They develop evidence-based guidelines for disease prevention, control, and treatment.

### Interdisciplinary Approaches to Disease Prevention

### *Collaboration Across Sectors*

*One Health Approach*

The One Health approach recognizes the interconnectedness of human, animal, and environmental health. It promotes collaboration among veterinarians, physicians, and environmental scientists to control zoonotic diseases (diseases that can spread between animals and humans).

*Zoonotic Disease Control*

Coordinated efforts to monitor and control diseases at the animal-human interface, such as avian influenza and rabies, prevent cross-species transmission.

*Environmental Surveillance*

Monitoring environmental factors, such as water quality and wildlife health, helps identify potential sources of outbreaks.

### Public-Private Partnerships

Public-private partnerships enhance resource mobilization, innovation, and implementation of health interventions. These partnerships bring together the strengths of both sectors to address public health challenges.

*Resource Allocation*

Private sector funding and expertise support public health initiatives, expanding their reach and impact.

*Innovation and Technology*

Collaborations with private companies foster the development of new technologies, such as diagnostic tools and vaccines.

### Research and Innovation

### Vaccine Development

Collaborative research efforts have led to the development of vaccines for diseases such as COVID-19, Ebola, and HPV. Continued research is essential for improving existing vaccines and developing new ones.

*Clinical Trials*

Rigorous clinical trials ensure the safety and efficacy of new vaccines before they are widely distributed.

*Global Collaboration*

International research partnerships accelerate vaccine development and distribution, especially during pandemics.

### Diagnostic Tools

Innovations in diagnostic technology, such as rapid tests and point-of-care diagnostics, enable quicker identification of infectious diseases. These tools are critical for early detection and timely intervention.

*Rapid Tests*

Point-of-care tests provide immediate results, facilitating prompt diagnosis and treatment.

*Molecular Diagnostics*

Techniques like PCR and next-generation sequencing offer high accuracy and specificity in detecting pathogens.

### Therapeutics

Research into new treatments and therapies, including antiviral drugs and monoclonal antibodies, improves patient outcomes and disease management. Innovative therapeutics can reduce the severity and duration of infections.

*Antiviral Drugs*

Development of new antiviral medications targets specific stages of viral replication, enhancing treatment efficacy.

*Monoclonal Antibodies*

These laboratory-produced molecules can mimic the immune system's response to pathogens, providing targeted treatment options.

**Policy and Regulation**

### Infection Control Guidelines

Policies on infection control in healthcare settings, such as hand hygiene protocols and isolation procedures, reduce the risk of disease transmission. These guidelines are based on evidence and best practices.

*Hand Hygiene*

Regular handwashing and use of hand sanitizers prevent the spread of pathogens in healthcare facilities.

*Isolation and Quarantine*

Implementing isolation procedures for infected individuals and quarantine measures for exposed individuals helps contain outbreaks.

### Travel Regulations

Policies related to travel, such as quarantine measures and vaccination requirements, help prevent the international spread of infectious diseases. These regulations are especially important during pandemics.

*Quarantine Measures*

Enforcing quarantine for travelers from affected regions reduces the risk of importing diseases.

*Vaccination Requirements*

Mandating vaccinations for travelers to and from certain areas prevents the spread of diseases like yellow fever.

### Environmental Regulations

Regulations addressing environmental factors, such as water quality standards and waste management, reduce the risk of disease outbreaks. Ensuring a clean and safe environment is crucial for public health.

*Water Quality Standards:*

Regulations to ensure safe drinking water prevent waterborne diseases such as cholera and typhoid.

*Waste Management:*

Proper disposal of waste, including medical and hazardous waste, prevents contamination and disease transmission.

**Public Awareness and Education Programs**

**Health Communication Strategies**

### *Mass Media Campaigns*

Television, radio, and print media are used to disseminate information about disease prevention, vaccination campaigns, and outbreak updates. Mass media reach a wide audience and can quickly convey important health messages.

*Awareness Campaigns:*

Campaigns raise awareness about the importance of vaccination, hygiene practices, and recognizing symptoms of infectious diseases.

*Behavior Change Communication:*

Media campaigns use persuasive techniques to encourage healthy behaviors and compliance with public health guidelines.

### *Digital and Social Media*

Social media platforms and websites provide real-time information and engage communities in health promotion activities. Digital media offer interactive and personalized communication channels.

*Social Media Engagement*

Platforms like Facebook, Twitter, and Instagram are used to share health tips, debunk myths, and provide updates on disease outbreaks.

Web-based Resources

Websites and mobile apps offer accessible information on disease prevention, symptoms, and treatment options.

### Community Outreach

### *Health Workers*

Health workers engage directly with communities through meetings, workshops, and door-to-door visits to educate and mobilize individuals. Community outreach ensures that health messages reach even the most remote areas.

*Workshops and Seminars*

Educational workshops provide detailed information on disease prevention and management, tailored to community needs.

*Door-to-Door Campaigns*

Health workers visit households to distribute information, answer questions, and encourage participation in health programs.

## School-Based Programs

### Curriculum Development

Health education curricula in schools cover topics such as hygiene, vaccination, sexual health, and disease prevention. Integrating health education into school curricula ensures that young people receive accurate and age-appropriate information.

*Comprehensive Health Education*

Programs include lessons on personal hygiene, nutrition, and the importance of vaccinations.

*Age-Appropriate Content*

Educational materials are tailored to different age groups to ensure relevance and understanding.

### School Health Services

Schools provide health services, including vaccinations and screenings, to promote student health and prevent disease transmission. These services are crucial for maintaining a healthy school environment.

*Vaccination Clinics*

Schools organize vaccination clinics to ensure students are immunized against common infectious diseases.

*Health Screenings*

Regular health screenings identify and address health issues early, preventing the spread of communicable diseases.

## Community Engagement

### Community Health Workers

Trained community members provide health education, support vaccination efforts, and facilitate access to healthcare services. Community health workers are trusted sources of information and play a key role in mobilizing communities.

*Local Outreach*

Community health workers engage with local residents, providing tailored health education and support.

*Vaccination Drives*

They assist in organizing and conducting vaccination campaigns, ensuring high coverage within communities.

### Participatory Approaches

Involving community members in planning and decision-making processes fosters ownership and enhances the effectiveness of interventions. Participatory approaches leverage local knowledge and resources.

*Community Advisory Boards*

Advisory boards comprising community representatives provide input on public health initiatives, ensuring they are culturally appropriate and effective.

*Participatory Planning*

Engaging communities in the design and implementation of health programs increases buy-in and sustainability.

## Behavioral Change Programs

### Social Marketing

Applying marketing principles to health promotion, social marketing campaigns encourage behaviors such as handwashing, safe sex practices, and vaccination. These campaigns use targeted messaging and behavior change theories to achieve their goals.

*Targeted Messaging*

Social marketing campaigns develop tailored messages to address specific behaviors and target populations.

*Multimedia Approaches*

Using various media channels, including print, digital, and social media, to reach and influence different audience segments.

### Nudge Theory

Behavioral economics principles, such as nudging, are used to design environments that encourage healthy choices without restricting freedom. Nudges subtly guide individuals towards healthier behaviors.

*Choice Architecture*

Designing environments that make healthy choices easier and more accessible, such as placing hand sanitizers at strategic locations.

*Incentives and Reminders*

Providing incentives for healthy behaviors and using reminders to reinforce positive actions, such as text message reminders for vaccinations.

### Peer Education

Peer educators share information and model healthy behaviors within their social networks, promoting behavior change through peer influence. Peer education is effective in reaching and influencing specific groups, such as adolescents and marginalized communities.

*Peer-led Workshops*

Trained peer educators conduct workshops and discussions on health topics, creating relatable and engaging learning experiences.

*Role Modeling*

Peer educators demonstrate healthy behaviors, encouraging others to adopt similar practices.

Public health plays a pivotal role in preventing and managing communicable diseases through robust infrastructure, interdisciplinary approaches, and effective public awareness and education programs. The success of these efforts relies on collaboration, innovation, and community engagement. As global health challenges continue to evolve, sustained investment in public health systems and ongoing commitment to disease prevention and control are essential for safeguarding public health and ensuring a healthier future for all. Through continuous improvement and adaptation, public health can effectively address the dynamic landscape of communicable diseases and protect communities worldwide.

# CHAPTER EIGHTEEN

# INTERNATIONAL EFFORTS AND ORGANIZATIONS COMBATING GLOBAL HEALTH THREATS

## 1. Introduction

Global health threats, such as pandemics, emerging infectious diseases, and persistent health disparities, necessitate a unified and coordinated international response. The collective efforts of various international organizations, collaborative initiatives, and strategies to address global health inequities play a pivotal role in safeguarding global health security. This chapter delves into the roles of key international organizations, highlights collaborative initiatives for enhancing global health security, and discusses approaches to addressing health disparities on a global scale.

## 2. Role of WHO and Other International Organizations

### 2.1 World Health Organization (WHO)

### 2.1.1 Overview and Mission

The World Health Organization (WHO), established in 1948 as a specialized agency of the United Nations, has a comprehensive mandate to promote health, keep the world safe, and serve the vulnerable. Its overarching goal is to ensure that all people attain the highest possible level of health. WHO's work is driven by its commitment to universal health coverage, health emergencies, and promoting healthier populations.

### 2.1.2 Key Functions and Responsibilities

- **Global Health Leadership:** WHO acts as a global leader in health, providing strategic direction and influencing health policy through evidence-based recommendations. It convenes stakeholders, fosters collaboration, and shapes the global health agenda.

- **Technical Support and Capacity Building:** WHO offers technical assistance to countries to strengthen their health systems. This includes providing expertise in health policy, planning, and management, as well as training health professionals to build local capacity.

- **Surveillance and Monitoring:** WHO operates a global surveillance system to monitor health trends and detect outbreaks early. This system includes the Global Outbreak Alert and Response Network (GOARN), which coordinates rapid response to international public health emergencies.

- **Health Guidelines and Standards:** WHO develops international health guidelines, standards, and protocols based on the latest scientific evidence. These include guidelines on disease prevention, treatment, and control measures, which member states are encouraged to adopt and implement.

## 2.2 Other Key International Organizations
### 2.2.1 United Nations Children's Fund (UNICEF)

UNICEF focuses on child health and well-being, advocating for the rights of children and providing support in areas such as nutrition, education, and emergency relief.

- **Immunization Programs:** UNICEF plays a crucial role in global immunization efforts, ensuring that children worldwide receive essential vaccines to protect against preventable diseases like measles, polio, and pneumonia.
- **Nutrition and WASH (Water, Sanitation, and Hygiene):** UNICEF's initiatives in promoting proper nutrition and ensuring access to clean water and sanitation are vital in preventing diseases, especially in vulnerable and underserved communities.

### 2.2.2 World Bank

The World Bank provides financial and technical support to countries to improve their health systems and address social determinants of health.

- **Health Financing:** The World Bank funds projects aimed at strengthening healthcare infrastructure, expanding access to health services, and improving health outcomes, particularly in low- and middle-income countries.

- **Policy Advice and Technical Assistance:** The World Bank offers policy advice and technical assistance to help countries design and implement effective health strategies, addressing issues such as health financing, service delivery, and health workforce development.

### 2.2.3 Global Fund to Fight AIDS, Tuberculosis and Malaria

The Global Fund mobilizes resources to combat AIDS, tuberculosis, and malaria, significantly contributing to the global fight against these diseases.

- **Funding and Grants:** The Global Fund provides grants to countries to scale up prevention, treatment, and care services for HIV/AIDS, tuberculosis, and malaria, with a focus on high-burden regions.
- **Public-Private Partnerships:** The Global Fund collaborates with governments, civil society, and the private sector to maximize the impact of its investments and ensure sustainable health outcomes.

### 2.2.4 GAVI, the Vaccine Alliance

GAVI works to increase access to immunization in low-income countries, ensuring that vaccines reach those most in need and contributing to global health security.

- **Vaccine Procurement and Distribution:** GAVI helps procure and distribute vaccines, improving immunization coverage and equity, and ensuring that life-saving vaccines are available to all children, regardless of where they live.

- **Health System Strengthening:** GAVI supports efforts to strengthen health systems, ensuring that they can deliver immunization services effectively and sustainably.

## 3. Collaborative Initiatives for Global Health Security
### 3.1 International Health Regulations (IHR)
### 3.1.1 Framework and Objectives

The International Health Regulations (IHR) are a legally binding framework established by WHO to help countries prevent, protect against, control, and provide a public health response to the international spread of diseases.

- **Core Capacities:** IHR requires countries to develop and maintain core capacities for surveillance, reporting, and responding to public health emergencies. This includes capacities for timely detection, assessment, and reporting of health events.
- **Notification and Coordination:** Countries must promptly notify WHO of public health events that may constitute a public health emergency of international concern (PHEIC), enabling a coordinated global response. The IHR also facilitate information sharing and collaboration between countries during health emergencies.

### 3.2 Global Health Security Agenda (GHSA)
### 3.2.1 Overview and Goals

The Global Health Security Agenda (GHSA) is a multilateral initiative launched in 2014 to enhance global health security through collaborative efforts among governments, international organizations, and the private sector.

- **Preventing Epidemics:** GHSA focuses on preventing the emergence and spread of infectious diseases by strengthening national health systems and promoting policies that reduce the risk of outbreaks.
- **Detecting Threats Early:** The initiative supports the development of robust surveillance systems, laboratory networks, and information sharing mechanisms to detect health threats early and respond effectively.
- **Responding Rapidly and Effectively:** GHSA promotes rapid response capabilities to mitigate the impact of health emergencies, including outbreak investigation, emergency preparedness, and response planning.

## 3.3 Public-Private Partnerships
### 3.3.1 Role and Benefits

Public-private partnerships leverage the strengths and resources of both sectors to address global health challenges, combining the innovation and efficiency of the private sector with the public sector's mandate and reach.

- **Pharmaceutical and Biotechnology Companies:** Collaborations with pharmaceutical companies accelerate the development, production, and distribution of vaccines, treatments, and diagnostics, ensuring timely access to essential medical products.
- **Non-Governmental Organizations (NGOs):** NGOs bring on-the-ground expertise and community connections, enhancing the implementation and effectiveness of health programs, especially in remote and underserved areas.

## 3.4 Research and Innovation Networks
### 3.4.1 Vaccine Development and Distribution

Global research networks facilitate the sharing of knowledge and resources to advance health innovations, including the development of vaccines for emerging infectious diseases.

- **Coalition for Epidemic Preparedness Innovations (CEPI):** CEPI funds the development of vaccines against diseases with epidemic potential, ensuring that vaccines can be rapidly developed and deployed during outbreaks.
- **Global Health Innovative Technology (GHIT) Fund:** The GHIT Fund supports the development of new health technologies and interventions for diseases that disproportionately affect low- and middle-income countries, fostering innovation and equitable access.

### 3.4.2 Diagnostic Tools and Therapeutics

Innovations in diagnostic technology and therapeutics are critical for early detection and effective treatment of infectious diseases.

- **Rapid Diagnostic Tests:** Point-of-care tests provide immediate results, facilitating prompt diagnosis and treatment, particularly in resource-limited settings.
- **Molecular Diagnostics:** Advanced techniques like PCR and next-generation sequencing offer high accuracy and specificity in detecting pathogens, supporting epidemiological surveillance and outbreak response.
- **Therapeutics Development:** Research into new treatments, including antiviral drugs and monoclonal antibodies, improves patient outcomes and enhances disease management, reducing the severity and duration of infections.

## 4. Addressing Health Disparities on a Global Scale
### 4.1 Social Determinants of Health
### 4.1.1 Economic Stability

Addressing economic stability is crucial for reducing health disparities and improving access to healthcare and healthy living conditions.

- **Poverty Reduction:** Efforts to reduce poverty through economic development, social protection programs, and inclusive growth strategies improve health outcomes and access to essential services.
- **Employment Opportunities:** Promoting decent work and fair wages enhances economic stability, enabling individuals and families to afford healthcare and healthy living conditions.

### 4.1.2 Education Access

Education empowers individuals with knowledge and skills to make informed health choices and access better opportunities.

- **Universal Education:** Ensuring access to quality education for all children, regardless of gender, socioeconomic status, or location, reduces health disparities and promotes healthier populations.
- **Health Literacy:** Integrating health education into school curricula enhances health literacy, enabling individuals to make informed decisions about their health and well-being.

### 4.1.3 Healthcare Access

Strengthening health systems and reducing barriers to healthcare access, such as cost and distance, improves health outcomes for marginalized populations.

- **Universal Health Coverage (UHC):** Implementing UHC ensures that all individuals have access to essential health services without financial hardship, reducing health disparities and promoting equity.
- **Primary Healthcare:** Strengthening primary healthcare systems ensures that communities have access to essential services, including preventive care, treatment, and health promotion.

### 4.2 Gender and Health Equity
### 4.2.1 Maternal and Child Health

Ensuring access to maternal and child health services reduces mortality and improves health outcomes for women and children.

- **Antenatal and Postnatal Care:** Providing comprehensive antenatal and postnatal care ensures the health and well-being of mothers and infants, reducing maternal and infant mortality rates.
- **Nutrition and Immunization:** Ensuring adequate nutrition and immunization for children promotes healthy growth and development, preventing common childhood illnesses.

### 4.2.2 Addressing Gender-Based Violence

Addressing gender-based violence through prevention and support services improves the health and well-being of affected individuals.

- **Prevention Programs:** Implementing programs to prevent gender-based violence, including education and awareness campaigns, reduces the incidence of violence and promotes gender equality.

- **Support Services:** Providing support services, such as counseling, legal assistance, and healthcare, helps survivors recover and rebuild their lives.

### 4.3 Global Health Initiatives
### 4.3.1 HIV/AIDS Programs

Global efforts to combat HIV/AIDS include prevention, treatment, and care services, particularly in high-burden regions.

- **Prevention Strategies:** Implementing prevention strategies, such as condom distribution, needle exchange programs, and pre-exposure prophylaxis (PrEP), reduces the transmission of HIV.
- **Treatment Access:** Ensuring access to antiretroviral therapy (ART) improves the health and longevity of people living with HIV, reducing morbidity and mortality.

### 4.3.2 Malaria Control Programs

Initiatives such as insecticide-treated bed nets and antimalarial drugs have significantly reduced malaria incidence and mortality.

- **Vector Control:** Implementing vector control measures, such as insecticide-treated bed nets and indoor residual spraying, reduces malaria transmission and protects vulnerable populations.
- **Diagnosis and Treatment:** Ensuring prompt diagnosis and effective treatment of malaria improves health outcomes and reduces the burden of the disease.

## 4.4 Health Systems Strengthening

### 4.4.1 Infrastructure and Workforce Development

Strengthening health systems involves improving infrastructure and developing a skilled health workforce.

- **Health Facilities:** Building and upgrading health facilities, particularly in rural and underserved areas, ensures that communities have access to essential health services.
- **Health Workforce:** Investing in the training and retention of health professionals, including doctors, nurses, and community health workers, enhances the capacity and quality of health services.

### 4.4.2 Health Information Systems

Robust health information systems are critical for monitoring health trends, managing health programs, and informing policy decisions.

- **Data Collection and Analysis:** Implementing systems for accurate and timely data collection and analysis supports evidence-based decision-making and program management.
- **Health Information Technology:** Leveraging health information technology, such as electronic health records and telemedicine, improves service delivery and patient outcomes.

International efforts and organizations play a pivotal role in combating global health threats and addressing health disparities. Through collaborative initiatives, policy frameworks, and targeted interventions, these entities work towards a healthier and more equitable world.

Sustained commitment, innovation, and cooperation are essential to ensure global health security and improve health outcomes for all. As global health challenges continue to evolve, the collective action of the international community remains crucial in safeguarding public health and promoting health equity worldwide.

# CHAPTER NINETEEN

# ETHICAL CONSIDERATIONS IN DISEASE CONTROL AND PREVENTION

## 1. Introduction

In the realm of disease control and prevention, ethical considerations hold significant importance. They guide decision-making processes that impact individuals, communities, and societies at large. This chapter delves into the intricate ethical dimensions inherent in disease control and prevention efforts, navigating the complex terrain of balancing individual rights with public health imperatives, addressing ethical challenges in research and practice, and fostering global cooperation guided by ethical principles.

## 2. Balancing Individual Rights with Public Health Measures

## 2.1 Autonomy vs. Public Health Mandates

### 2.1.1 Informed Consent

Informed consent stands as a cornerstone of ethical medical practices, ensuring individuals understand the risks and benefits associated with medical interventions and research participation. However, during public health crises, the need for swift action sometimes clashes with the meticulous process of securing individual consent.

## 2.2 Privacy and Confidentiality

### 2.2.1 Data Collection and Surveillance

While public health surveillance systems rely on gathering personal health data to monitor disease trends and implement control measures, protecting individuals' privacy and confidentiality is paramount to maintaining trust and respecting autonomy.

## 2.3 Equity and Social Justice

### 2.3.1 Vulnerable Populations

Addressing health disparities and promoting social justice require equitable access to healthcare services and resources, particularly for marginalized and vulnerable populations. Ethical considerations underscore the imperative to prioritize their needs and tackle underlying systemic inequalities.

## 3. Ethical Challenges in Research and Public Health Practice

### 3.1 Research Ethics

### 3.1.1 Informed Consent and Risk-Benefit Assessment

Research endeavors in infectious diseases demand rigorous adherence to ethical standards, including obtaining informed consent from participants and conducting thorough risk-benefit assessments to ensure the welfare of research subjects.

## 3.2 Allocation of Resources

### 3.2.1 Scarce Resource Allocation

During crises, such as pandemics or natural disasters, the ethical allocation of limited resources becomes imperative. Ethical principles of justice guide decision-making to ensure fairness and maximize benefits across affected populations.

### 3.3 Public Health Interventions

### 3.3.1 Coercive Measures and Individual Rights

The implementation of coercive measures, such as quarantine or mandatory vaccination, necessitates careful consideration of individual rights and liberties. Ethical justification for such measures hinges on necessity, proportionality, and respect for individual autonomy.

### 4. Global Cooperation and Ethical Guidelines

### 4.1 International Collaboration

### 4.1.1 Sharing of Data and Resources

Global solidarity and cooperation are indispensable in combating transnational health threats. Ethical considerations underpin the sharing of data and resources to ensure equitable access to interventions and promote collective well-being.

### 4.2 Ethical Guidelines and Standards

### 4.2.1 WHO Ethical Guidance

The World Health Organization (WHO) provides ethical frameworks to guide decision-making in public health emergencies and research. These guidelines emphasize principles of respect, equity, transparency, and accountability.

### 4.3 Multilateral Agreements and Treaties

### 4.3.1 International Health Regulations (IHR)

Multilateral agreements, such as the International Health Regulations (IHR), establish legal frameworks for international cooperation in disease surveillance and response. Ethical considerations, including respect for human rights and minimizing disruptions to international trade, inform these agreements.

Ethical considerations serve as guiding lights in the multifaceted landscape of disease control and prevention. They underscore the delicate balance between individual rights and public health imperatives, navigate ethical challenges in research and practice, and foster global cooperation grounded in ethical principles. By upholding ethical standards, stakeholders can navigate complex ethical dilemmas and steer toward a future where health equity and well-being are upheld as universal values.

# CHAPTER TWENTY

# EMERGING CHALLENGES IN THE FIELD OF COMMUNICABLE DISEASES

In the dynamic realm of communicable diseases, staying ahead of emerging challenges is paramount for effective disease control and prevention. This chapter explores the multifaceted landscape of emerging threats, delving into strategies for anticipation, the transformative role of technology, and the profound impact of climate change on disease dynamics.

## 1. Anticipating and Addressing New Threats

### 1.1 Surveillance and Early Warning Systems

Rapid detection of emerging infectious diseases hinges on robust surveillance and early warning systems. These systems, fortified by advances in data analytics and international collaboration, enable the timely identification of novel pathogens and potential disease outbreaks. By monitoring disease trends, tracking unusual patterns, and sharing information globally, public health authorities can swiftly respond to emerging threats before they escalate into widespread epidemics.

## 1.2 One Health Approach

The One Health approach recognizes the interconnectedness of human, animal, and environmental health in the emergence and spread of infectious diseases. By integrating expertise from diverse disciplines, including medicine, veterinary science, ecology, and environmental science, stakeholders can anticipate and address emerging zoonotic diseases more effectively. Through collaborative research, surveillance, and intervention efforts, the One Health approach fosters a holistic understanding of disease dynamics and facilitates proactive measures to mitigate emerging threats at their source.

## 1.3 Global Preparedness and Response

Effective preparedness and response to new disease threats require coordinated global efforts and resilient health systems. By investing in surveillance infrastructure, laboratory capacity, and workforce training, nations can enhance their readiness to detect and contain outbreaks. International collaboration, guided by frameworks such as the International Health Regulations (IHR), enables the rapid sharing of information, resources, and expertise during public health emergencies. By working together, the global community can strengthen its collective ability to respond to emerging threats and safeguard public health worldwide.

## 2. Technology and its Role in Disease Control

## 2.1 Digital Surveillance and Epidemiology

Advancements in digital surveillance and epidemiological tools revolutionize disease control efforts by providing real-time insights into disease dynamics. By harnessing big data, artificial intelligence, and geographic information systems, public health authorities can monitor disease trends, detect outbreaks early, and target interventions more effectively. Digital platforms facilitate rapid data sharing, enabling collaborative responses across borders and improving the efficiency of disease control efforts.

## 2.2 Telemedicine and Remote Healthcare Delivery

Telemedicine emerges as a vital tool in disease control, particularly during public health emergencies and in remote or underserved areas. By leveraging teleconsultations, mobile health applications, and remote monitoring technologies, healthcare providers can deliver essential services to patients without the need for in-person visits. Telemedicine enhances access to care, improves patient outcomes, and reduces the burden on healthcare infrastructure, especially in resource-constrained settings or during times of crisis.

## 2.3 Vaccine Development and Novel Therapeutics

Technological innovations drive progress in vaccine development and the discovery of novel therapeutics for emerging infectious diseases. Platforms such as mRNA vaccines and viral vector-based vaccines offer unprecedented speed and flexibility in vaccine development, enabling rapid responses to new disease threats. Additionally, advances in antiviral therapies, monoclonal antibodies, and immune-based treatments expand treatment options and improve outcomes for individuals infected with novel pathogens.

## 3. The Impact of Climate Change on Disease Dynamics

### 3.1 Vector-Borne Diseases

Climate change influences the distribution, behavior, and abundance of vectors, such as mosquitoes and ticks, leading to shifts in the epidemiology of vector-borne diseases. Rising temperatures, altered precipitation patterns, and changes in habitat suitability create favorable conditions for vector proliferation and disease transmission. By understanding the complex interactions between climate, ecology, and vector-borne diseases, public health authorities can develop targeted strategies for surveillance, vector control, and community education to mitigate the impact of climate change on disease dynamics.

### 3.2 Waterborne and Foodborne Diseases

Climate variability affects water quality, availability, and sanitation infrastructure, influencing the transmission of waterborne and foodborne diseases. Extreme weather events, such as floods and droughts, can compromise water sources, contaminate food supplies, and disrupt sanitation systems, increasing the risk of disease outbreaks. By implementing measures to improve water and sanitation infrastructure, strengthen food safety protocols, and enhance public awareness, communities can reduce the burden of waterborne and foodborne diseases exacerbated by climate change.

### 3.3 Infectious Disease Resurgence

Climate-related environmental changes, including deforestation, urbanization, and habitat destruction, create ecological disruptions that impact disease dynamics. The disruption of ecosystems can lead to the emergence or resurgence of infectious diseases, including zoonoses and novel pathogens. By addressing environmental degradation, promoting sustainable land use practices, and enhancing surveillance and response capacities, communities can mitigate the risk of infectious disease resurgence driven by climate change.

Navigating the complex landscape of emerging challenges in communicable diseases requires a multifaceted approach that integrates anticipation, innovation, and collaboration. By strengthening surveillance systems, leveraging technology, and addressing the impacts of climate change, stakeholders can enhance their readiness to detect, respond to, and mitigate emerging threats. Through concerted efforts at the local, national, and global levels, we can build resilient health systems capable of effectively addressing the evolving challenges posed by communicable diseases in the 21st century.